How to write a
nonfiction book

how to
write

From planning
to promotion
in 6 simple steps

7th EDITION

a nonfiction book

BOBBI LINKEMER

LinkUp Publishing

How to Write a Nonfiction Book:
From planning to promotion in 6 simple steps
Seventh Edition

© 2011 by Bobbi Linkemer. All rights reserved

ISBN: 978-0-9826746-6-6
Library of Congress Control Number: 2011942029

Cover designed by Nehmen-Kodner: www.n-kcreative.com
Written by Bobbi Linkemer
Published & Distributed by LinkUp Publishing
St. Louis, Missouri

WriteANonfictionBook.com
bobbi@writeanonfictionbook.com
PO Box 440023
St. Louis, Missouri 63144

Dedicated to

my students, clients,
and readers
who have taught me so much

OTHER BOOKS BY BOBBI LINKEMER

Words To Live By
Reflections on the writing life from a 40-year veteran

Going Solo: How to Survive & Thrive as a Freelance Writer
(Now an e-book)

Invisible Author: Confessions of a Ghostwriter (e-book)

The Secretary's Secret Weapon:
Arm Yourself With 7 Essential Communication Skills

(Revised and republished as) *Shoptalk: 6 ways to get your*
message across at work (now an e-book)

Secretária Eficiente: Prepare-se para o successo Desenvolva
as sete habilidades essenciais de communicação

Dealing with Difficult People
(Published in the U.S. as *Solving People Problems*)

Polish Your People Skills

Get Organized, with Rene Richards

Planning and Running Effective Meetings
(A self-study course)

How to Write an Effective Resume

Polish Your Professional Image

How to Run a Meeting

Let's Talk:
People With Developmental Disabilities Speak Out

Change is Good! Stories of Community Inclusion

If the desire to write is not accompanied by actual writing, then the desire is not to write.
—Hugh Prather

There is no perfect time to write. There's only now.
—Barbara Kingsolver

Writing is an exploration. You start from nothing and learn as you go.
—E.L. Doctorow

There is no rule on how to write. Sometimes it comes easily and perfectly; sometimes it's like drilling rock.
—Ernest Hemingway

CONTENTS

INTRODUCTION

I can hardly believe I am writing the seventh edition of this book, which started out as an eight-and-a-half-by-eleven-inch workbook with only thirty-six pages. The copyright says 2004, and the subject matter was almost entirely about how to write a proposal. That was the first year I taught my class at the St. Louis Community College titled "Writing, Publishing, and Promoting Your Nonfiction Book." The classes have been a joy to teach, and with each one, I have learned from my students and the wonderful speakers who volunteered their time to share their knowledge and experience. I have shamelessly incorporated those lessons into each new edition of the book.

Not only have I learned and taught new skills, but I have also applied them to my own life. Last year, I decided to test the process I was teaching by planning, writing, and

< 1 >

promoting a book on my blog, "The Writing Life." What I wanted to know was, does this process work? The bottom line is it *does* work. Having said that, I must add that going through all of the steps in this book is not for the faint of heart. It takes dedication, determination, and discipline. It takes love of your subject and effort. Books do not write themselves. They are not the product of inspiration and magic. They are the result of planning and much hard work. But when you hold your tangible, published book in your hand, you will know it was worth every minute of time you spent on it.

Here is indisputable proof that this process works. The following books have been written by students or clients who applied its principles to their books.

- *Amazing Journey: Metamorphosis of a Hidden Child* by Felicia Graber
- *A Return to Abundance* by Paul L. Gubany
- *Beyond the Ice Cream Cone: The Whole Scoop on Food at the 1904 World's Fair* by Pamela J. Vaccaro
- *Crash & Burn: The Bureaupathology of the Federal Aviation Administration* by Robert M. Misic
- *Dressing Nifty After Fifty: The Definitive Guide to a Simple, Stylish Wardrobe* by Corinne Richardson
- *From Red Star to Spangled Banner* by Dale Atilla Fogarasi
- *It's Your Life, Choose Well* by Kathleen Keller Passanisi
- *Keys to Revelation: Messages in Letters, Symbols, and Patterns* by Rev. Donald R. Meisner

< 2 >

- *Mood Blitz: Bipolar Disorder, an Onslaught of Mania and Depression* by Marti Markley
- *Who's Been Sleeping in My Bed(room)? Researching a St. Louis County, Missouri Home* by Kim Wolterman

What should you know?

- Books are a labor of love. The first thing you must love is your subject. It has to be something you are compelled to share with others. If you are casual about it, you won't make it through the long haul. Think of writing an article as a sprint; that makes writing a book a marathon.
- Sitting down to write when the spirit moves you is what I call "starting in the middle." A nonfiction book takes planning. Planning is a lot of work but worth the effort because every single bit of your plan will eventually find its way into your book or promotional activities.
- If you have never written a book, the process seems mysterious and maybe even impossible. It is neither. It's logical and orderly. If you doubt it, reread the list of titles on the previous page.
- All along the route from start to finish, there are choices to be made. Some are small: Should I write in first person or third? Should I stick to present tense or use past tense? Some are more complicated: Should I try to find an agent who may sell my book to a traditional publisher, or should I publish it myself? If I do it myself, should I start my own publishing company or use a print on demand (POD) firm?

< 3 >

- Once the book is published, it is your job to promote it, and you should have been thinking about how you would do that from the very beginning. This is not the time to start your marketing campaign.
- The best part of being an author should be the process, not the end result.

Do you have a book in you?

It seems almost everyone I meet harbors a secret—or not-so-secret—yearning to write a book. Ideas range from memoirs to mysteries, from pamphlets to tomes. I am very popular at cocktail parties when people hear that I'm an author. They can't wait to tell me all about their books, though I find that very few people are able to explain what their books are about in one or two sentences. They ramble on and on but can't seem to get to the heart of the matter.

When would-be authors ask me questions, they usually want to know (in fifty words or less) how to write a book or if I would mind taking a look at their work and telling them what I think. This book is in response to the first question, and I am learning to answer no to the second. People really don't want to know what I think unless it's glowing praise. When I read something that cries out for editing, it takes a great deal of self-control to forgo the red pen. And when I do succumb and begin doing what comes naturally, the writer is usually insulted. Now, when people ask me to read their books or send me an unsolicited manuscript, I tell them my hourly rate. It tends to throw a damper on the conversation.

< 4 >

Writing a book is not rocket science, but it is hard work. While people who get all the way through the process know this is true, aspiring authors may not realize just how much work is involved. It sounds a bit glamorous to be a published author, and to a degree it is. Just imagine holding your first book in your hands and seeing your name on the cover. I will admit I still find it thrilling.

People write books for many reasons. Some love the process (I am one who does); others know the benefits and think they are well worth the effort; still others take on the challenge because their audiences or constituencies expect them to.

Why should you write your book?

There are as many reasons to write a book as there are books. Here are just a few of the most compelling. Whether you are truly an authority on a subject or not, just put that subject between book covers, and people will assume you must be. After all, only experts write books. True? Well, no, but the myth persists. So, you might as well ride the wave. If you are an expert, all the better. You will really have something worth writing… and reading.

Credibility is only one reason. If you do a good job of promoting your book, you may actually make money on it. Let me offer a caveat here: Writing books does not guarantee that you will get rich quick, or at all. It takes an enormous amount of time and effort to market a book successfully. Few people have any idea what Mark Victor Hansen and Jack Canfield—the authors of the first *Chicken Soup for the*

< 5 >

Soul—did before their book took off. Their faith in the quality of their product was unshakable, but it took more than faith to create a best seller that launched an industry.

When you know your topic and want to share what you know with others, a book is one of the best ways to do it. More and more professional speakers are selling their books in the back of the room after their presentations. A product—a book, a CD, or a DVD—captures their subject matter and commands higher speaking fees.

High-profile CEOs often write books to pass along their business philosophies and practices to the next generation of leaders in their organizations; to articulate to significant stakeholders their personal visions for their companies; or to apply the hard-won lessons of their lives to the broader context of business, society, academia, or government.

What's holding you back?

If I ask you whether you have a book out or in the works, and the answer is, "No, not yet..." I can't help wondering why not. I can almost hear the answers: *I wouldn't know where to begin... Writing a book is just too overwhelming to think about... My plate is so full; I simply don't have the time.*

Whatever your excuses, I've heard them all. What if I told you that you could write a book in six months... *if* you stuck to a program? You can, but only with a plan and some tenacity. This book is the plan; you will have to supply the tenacity.

All big projects seem overwhelming when you view them

< 6 >

in their totality. Mountain climbers preparing to climb the Himalayas don't expect to do it all in a single day. They have a plan, and they execute it one day at a time. More accurately, they do it one step at a time, and that is exactly how you write a book.

Finally, let me shatter the mystique associated with writing a book. Anything you do for the first time has an element of mystery, simply because you haven't done it before, but one step inside any bookstore will clearly demonstrate how many thousands of people have solved the mystery. Granted, not all the books on the shelves are good, but somehow, they were not only written but published as well.

What does it take to write a book?

1. Desire
2. A concept
3. A plan
4. A long attention span
5. Self-discipline
6. Support and guidance

Desire, of course, means that you really want to write this book. Now that it's beginning to crystallize in your mind, your excitement for your topic is mounting. At this point in the process, my desire usually turns into obsession. I can't think about anything else. I can't wait to get started. Obsession is the beginning of self-motivation, but, like an exercise program that starts out with a bang, self-motivation takes work. Here's where you have to ask yourself

< 7 >

whether this book is going to be a catharsis of the soul, a hobby, or a project that might actually make some money. That is one powerful test of your idea. Would anyone (besides your mother) want to read it, and would that person actually part with money to own it? She believed in *Harry Potter* when no one else did, and her phenomenal success made her an icon and a millionaire many times over.

The key to any book is the strength of its **concept,** its point. If you can't explain what your book is in one sentence, you don't have a clear idea of your message. In the early stages of my writing career, when I got stuck on an article, my twelve-year-old daughter would ask, "What is it about, Mom? And keep it short." It was good training.

I know this is a cliché, but just as you wouldn't set out on a road trip without a road map, you don't start a book without **a plan**. This is where many first-time authors go wrong. They have the romantic idea that one begins a book by sitting down at the computer and just "letting it flow." If you ever hope to get all the way through this process, you have to have a plan.

Writing a book requires focus and commitment over many months. That's called a **long attention span.** Think of it as tying a knot on one end of a hot pink thread at the beginning of the process and pulling that thread all the way through the planning, writing, publishing, and promoting of your book. The more excited you are about your book and the more determined you are to see it come to fruition, the more likely you are to remain focused every tiny step of the way.

< 8 >

If you've ever tried to diet, you know how hard it can be to maintain your determination to cut calories. **Self-discipline** is doing what has to be done, sticking with it even when it's not fun, and reasserting your commitment as often as necessary.

No one goes it alone, especially when you undertake a project of this magnitude. No matter which book you're working on—your first or twenty-first—you need to feel that others are in your corner and rooting for you. That's **support.** Not only do *you* need faith in your subject, you also need *others* to have faith in you.

If this is your first book, **guidance** from a knowledgeable source is a gift. Guidance comes in many forms and from many sources—teachers, fellow writers, writers' groups, writing classes, and professionals—especially book-writing coaches.

How can a book coach help you?

1. **A book coach is a teacher, partner, and personal cheerleader.** You may not even know when you begin how much you need someone to fill those roles. But these are the secret ingredients of success when you tackle a book project for the first time. There are many places along this path when your enthusiasm or confidence may falter. A book coach will help you stay focused and sure of yourself over the long haul.

2. **A book coach guides you through every step of the process.** If you are like most new authors, you may be so eager to write that you just sit down and start. There

< 9 >

is a prescribed process for writing a nonfiction book, which is covered in the planning section of this book on page 25.

3. **A book coach asks all the right questions during the planning phase.** These are the questions you must be able to answer before you begin writing. The most important, of course, is, What is the subject of your book?

4. **A book coach helps you set realistic goals and create a schedule for meeting them.** Writing a book is a long-term project but certainly not one that should drag on forever. It is essential to set achievable goals to mark your progress along the way. Like all good goals, these should be specific and measurable and have firm completion dates.

5. **A book coach works with you on polishing your manuscript.** Regular feedback from your coach during the writing process will not only keep you on track, it will also provide an objective and knowledgeable outside perspective. When you have written your last word, saved the file, and printed out your manuscript, you will know it is the best it can be.

6. **A book coach clarifies available publishing options.** You may start out dreaming of having a large New York publisher make sure your book goes on the new nonfiction table of every bookstore, and that may be entirely possible. But conventional publishing is not for everyone or every book, and your coach can make you aware of all of the other viable options for putting your book between covers.

< 10 >

7. **A book coach helps you promote your book before and after it is published.** Whether you are snapped up by the best known of the "big houses" or start your own publishing company, much, if not all, of the marketing and promotion is going to be your responsibility. This is news to many first-time authors. Ideally, marketing should be a strategic part of your planning from the very beginning.

One last possibility

What if you are not a writer and you know it… or you are really too busy to write… or you honestly would rather drink castor oil than try to write a book? Well, you have a problem, but every problem has a solution. While I hesitate to give you this escape clause, you *could* work with a ghostwriter.

In essence, a ghostwriter becomes your voice for one purpose: to express your thoughts and ideas as you wish them to be read by others. A ghostwriter has a special knack for crawling inside your head, understanding what you want to say, and speaking in your voice.

What is ghostwriting?

Ghostwriting is a form of freelance writing. In other words, it is a business transaction, and a ghostwriter is a supplier of services. As the client, you pay for those services and have full control over the copy. Terms and details are agreed upon before you start the project. You have a right to expect the

< 11 >

ghostwriter to perform professionally and to respect confidentiality.

What does a ghostwriter write?

- **Books:** For an organization, a book is a highly specialized and often expensive form of business communication, but in many cases, the payback can be enormous. Individuals, too, hire ghostwriters for all of the reasons mentioned above.

- **Corporate histories:** Businesses are like families: They have personalities, cultures, and histories. Publicly owned companies tell their stories in annual reports; private companies have fewer regulatory restrictions and thus much more freedom in how they tell theirs.

- **Family histories:** People want to connect with their roots. In a society where grandparents no longer live down the block and extended families are often neighbors instead of relatives, more people than ever want to capture their stories while there are still people around who remember them.

- **Memoirs and autobiographies:** Everyone has a story to tell, which is one reason writing classes are full of people who want to put their stories between the covers of books. From tell-all memoirs to discreet, thoughtful autobiographies, these books sell well and, sometimes, even dispel the stigma surrounding many sensitive topics (alcoholism, drug addiction, and abuse, to name a few). It is

< 12 >

one thing to know your own story; it is quite another to write it coherently and colorfully.

- **Proposals:** There are three main types of proposals—business proposals, book proposals, and grants. All of them are like resumes; they get you in the door. They also force you to think through every aspect of your project and spell it out in concise, coherent language.

In the following chapters I will take you through the six steps to publication. Chapter 1 is an overview of what's to come, and Chapters 2-5 provide the details. When you're done with this book, you will be well on your way to becoming a published author.

< 13 >

THE PROCESS

1. Planning

What it is

Planning is the first and most important step in the process. For many authors, it is also the most difficult because it forces them to ask themselves many tough questions. Strangely, one of the toughest is also one of the simplest. If you were to submit your book to a publisher, the most important question you would be expected to answer is "What is the subject of your book?"

Why it's important

Even if you plan to self-publish, writing a proposal organizes your thoughts and helps you plan every aspect of your non-fiction book. Will it stand up to the competition? Where

< 15 >

would it go in a bookstore? Who is going to read it? Why would they want to read it? Do you really have a book here, or should you just write an article and get it out of your system? A proposal is your thinking document—a work in progress—until the moment you send it off to an agent or publisher. It is much more than a mere exercise because almost every word of it will become a part of the book later on. Don't make the mistake of skipping this step.

What it contains

A proposal must answer several basic questions. While the form of the proposal may vary and the answers may be in a different order, the basic information must be there. Most often, the proposal is arranged in the following categories:

- Concept statement
- About the book
- About the author
- About the market
- About the competition
- Production details
- About promotion
- Table of contents
- Chapter summaries
- Sample chapters

II. Writing

What it is

This is the heart of the matter, the content, and the reason you are writing this book. It is the most time-consuming part

< 16 >

of the process and what most people are talking about when they say, "I'm writing a book."

Why it's important

Your subject is very important to you. You know a lot about it, because you have either researched it or experienced it. You want to share it with others in a way that moves them, changes them, entertains them, or teaches them something. You want your readers not only to get your message but also to respond to it.

What it contains

The book comprises four parts:

1. Covers
- Front cover
- Back cover

2. Front Matter
- Copyright page
- Dedication page
- Foreword
- Preface
- Acknowledgments
- Introduction

3. Main Content
- Chapters

< 17 >

4. Back Matter

- Appendices
- Glossary
- Bibliography
- Index

III. Professional Partners

What it is

Professional partners are all the people who will play a role in some aspect of your book. They include everyone from editors to indexers and from proofreaders to publicists. While there are many potential partners on the list, you are unlikely to need all of them. Whom you choose depends on many factors: how elaborate your book will be, how you plan to publish, how much money you have to spend, and what part of the promotion you will do yourself.

Why it's important

Very few people can, or would even want to, do everything that must be done to take a book from concept to completion, especially if completion includes marketing. This requires a team of people, each with an area of specialization and all focused on a single outcome—making your book a success.

What it contains

This part of the process contains a list of resources and how these possible professional partners can augment your efforts. Here are some of them:

< 18 >

- Administrative or virtual assistant
- Attorney
- Calligrapher
- Content editor
- Copy editor
- Cover designer
- Developmental editor
- Distributor
- Illustrator
- Indexer
- Page-layout designer
- Printer
- Publicist
- Reviewers
- Social media expert
- Transcriber
- Typographer
- Web designer
- Wholesaler

IV. Production

What it is

Between the completed manuscript and the published book is a series of activities handled by conventional and independent publishers or by you, if you self-publish. If you are new to publishing, production details may seem confusing at first, but many of them are just a matter of preference or straightforward facts, e.g., number of pages, program used to create the manuscript (word-processing or layout), format

< 19 >

in which you will submit (high-resolution PDF, layout, or word processing), and whether there will be photographs or illustrations. If you are self-publishing, this list includes many other details, such as binding, paper, type style, and number of copies.

Why it's important

Why do you pick up a book on a table full of books? What makes you reach for one book on a shelf when all you can see is the spine? What catches your eye as you thumb through the pages? Do you like the size of the book or the feel of the paper or the type style, or do you feel a lack of connection and put the book back where you found it? Someone made those decisions, and someone brought them to life. No matter how you publish, you will play a role in those decisions.

What it contains

- Back matter
- Book length
- Cover design
- Endorsements
- Front matter
- Interior design
- Permissions
- Printer
- Printing specs
- Resources needed to complete your book
- Photographs and artwork

< 20 >

- Sidebars
- Submission program
- Type style

V. Publishing

What it is

Publishing is the step that converts digital files or plates into printed, bound pages between two covers. In other words, when the publishing step is complete, you can finally hold your book in your hands. One exception is electronic publishing. An e-book is no less real but certainly less tangible.

Why it's important

Your book exists to convey a message, but to accomplish its purpose, it must be in a form readers can access. Publishing is the step that enables people to read it, but it also requires a unique set of skills. There are many more options for authors than there were years ago when the choices were limited to conventional publishing houses and vanity press. Traditional publishing still exists, but it is only one of several options available to you. The more you know about those options, the better equipped you are to make the right choice.

What it contains

There are six publishing options:

1. Conventional or traditional
2. Self-publishing
3. Print-on-demand (POD)

< 21 >

4. Independent publishing
5. Electronic publishing
6. Do nothing

VI. Promotion

What it is

Your book has been published. Your challenge now is to get the copies out of your basement or warehouse and into the hands of readers. To do that, you have to let your target audience know it exists. This should *not* be the point at which you start thinking about how to do that. In fact, the time to consider your promotional strategy is during the planning phase. If you wrote a proposal, you have already outlined the steps you will take to help your publisher promote your book or to assume full responsibility for doing it yourself if you are self-publishing.

Why it's important

Walk into any bookstore, and you will see how many books are vying for readers' attention. In your genre, which is nonfiction, there are thousands upon thousands. This is not meant to discourage you but to help you see that if you don't let your readers know your book is waiting to be read, it will be lost in the crowd. Letting them know is called *promotion.*

What it contains

Here are some ways to promote your book:
• Advance readers copies

< 22 >

- Advertising
- Amazon.com
- Articles
- Blogging
- Book clubs
- Book fairs
- Elevator speech
- Internet marketing
- Networking
- Nontraditional sales
- Public relations
- Social media
- Speaking

< 23 >

STEP 1: PLANNING

roposals are important, but they can also be intimidating. If you can answer the following ten questions, you can write a book proposal. In fact, the answers to these questions may be all the proposal you need if you are going to self-publish. At the end of each question is a note about where the answer will go in your proposal.

Ten Questions to Test Your Book Idea

(For an online form to answer these questions, go to http://www.writeanonfictionbook.com/Client_Questionnaire.doc.)

1. Why are you writing this book? What do you hope to achieve? *(Marketing Plan)*

< 25 >

2. What is your book about (in one or two sentences)?
You must answer it before you go any further. You can't write a book if you don't know what it's about! (*Concept Statement and Marketing Plan*)

3. How are you qualified to write this book? This is your bio as it pertains to your subject. It demonstrates your knowledge, experience, and expertise. (*About the Author*)

4. Why is this an appropriate and timely topic? What is the big picture? The context? The political or social environment? Why this book, now? (*About the Book*)

5. Who is your ideal reader? Describe this person demographically and by interests. What do you know about him or her? (*About the Market and Marketing Plan*)

6. How will your reader benefit? Why should he read it? What will she learn? What problem will it solve? (*About the Market, Audience*)

7. How will you reach your ideal reader? What does he read, do, like? Where is she likely to buy this book? Amazon. com? In the grocery store? From your website? In a bookstore? (*About the Market*)

8. How big is the market? How many potential readers are there? (Make a list of publications your ideal reader prefers and add up the circulation figures; list organizations

< 26 >

she belongs to and estimated membership.) *(About the Market)*

9. What else is out there on this subject? Be specific about titles. How is this book unique/special/important? This is more than just a list; it is an analysis of how the competition's books compare to yours. *(About the Competition)*

10. How will you help to promote your book? Delineate specific plans. You need a plan that allows publishers to assess your willingness and cooperation in promoting your book. Publishers also want to evaluate your connections. This is called your "platform." *(About Promotion)*

Writing Your Proposal

Now that you have answered those ten important questions, the more formal proposal should be a snap. Here are a few hints. What follows is an explanation of each section of the proposal; the chart on the following page is a graphic depiction of how it all fits together. As you can see, you will have to write about the author, the market, the competition, production, and promotion before you can consolidate those sections in a brief, easily readable, and persuasive *About the Book* section.

The concept statement

While it is the first thing an editor will see and read, it is the last thing you write. Why? Because the **Concept Statement** is the encapsulation of the entire proposal. Thus, it cannot

< 27 >

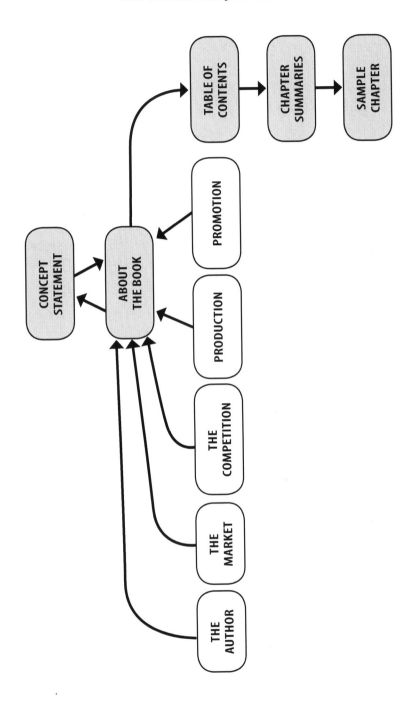

< 28 >

be written until the proposal has been completed and all of your information is assembled and entered.

About the book

The next-to-last section you write is a detailed description of the book from which the **Concept Statement** will be drawn; it cannot be written all at once. As each segment is fleshed out and clarified, it can be threaded into **About the Book** and refined later. Each question requires a short version of what you have written elsewhere in the proposal. For example, the question "What else is out there on the subject?" depends on the information in **About the Competition.** It's easy to think you can answer these questions before you do the necessary research, but it makes for a far more effective proposal if you think through each part and then transfer the information to **About the Book.** To make that easier, this section appears right after the **Concept Statement**.

After you answer all the questions in **About the Book,** you will have to organize and polish the answers according to one or two formats. One starts with the big picture and ends with the book; the other is just the opposite. These appear on page 39.

About the Author

This section contains your bio, with particular emphasis on your qualifications to write the book. This is the place to demonstrate your knowledge, experience, and expertise in

< 29 >

relation to your subject. What makes you the ideal person to convey this information? What is the thread that connects you to your topic? (You have already answered this in your ten questions, so you can simply cut and paste.)

About your ideal reader

This is the person you imagine as you write. How do you identify this person? Start by asking yourself who is attending your presentations or visiting your website? If you teach, who are your students? Who comments on your blog? If you have clients, who are they? Who would benefit from your information? Describe this person. As you begin to define your market, include as many of these characteristics as possible:

- Gender, if appropriate
- Approximate age
- Education level
- Socioeconomic level
- Media (what he watches, reads, listens to)
- Entertainment (what she does for fun)

About the market

This section requires research and is probably one of the most time-consuming, yet necessary, ones in the proposal. If you have colleagues who have written and marketed books, ask them for advice. Begin by defining a category, such as self-help or autobiography, that indicates where the book belongs in the bookstore. This section must answer the following questions:

< 30 >

- How large is the market? How many potential readers are there?
- What publications are they reading? What is the circulation of the publications they are reading?
- What organizations do they belong to? How many members does each organization have?
- What trends can be supported statistically?
- How many books are sold annually by subject (see the *Bowker Annual Library and Book Trade Almanac*)
- How can this market be reached? Where are readers likely to buy this book? Consider the following:
  1. Bookstores
  2. Book sections in grocery stores and specialty stores
  3. Institutional sales (public libraries, university ibraries and bookstores)
  4. Special sales and subsidiary sales (See *Literary Market Place* for lists of book clubs.)
  5. Locations applicable to your subject

About the competition

This section should answer these questions or address these issues:

- What does the audience need from this book?
- What problem will it help solve?
- What do existing books on the subject cover or not cover?
- If there is nothing like this book on the market, why has no one tackled this subject?

< 31 >

Sources include amazon.com, bn.com, Google or your favorite search engine, and of course, bricks-and-mortar bookstores. Don't be concerned if you find that your topic is not unique. There are very few unique topics. What matters is how you approach it, calling upon your own stories, research, experience, knowledge, and creativity. Be specific. List major competitive titles and a very brief description of each.

Production details

This is not a subject with which most writers are familiar, but it is helpful in terms of designing the book. Production details include the following:

- Book length: rounded off in double-spaced pages or word count
- Delivery date: expressed in three-month increments or upon receipt of an advance
- Type of computer and word-processing program; format of submission
- Format: special preferences in size, binding, font
- Sidebars: estimated number and content
- Permissions: how many, from whom, actual or estimated fees
- Front matter: preface, foreword, introduction, dedication, acknowledgments
- Back matter: index, bibliography, resource directory, glossary, appendices
- Endorsements: who is committed or whom to contact
- Resources needed to complete your book: itemized

< 32 >

expenses, travel, long-distance calls, permissions, editing
- Photographs and artwork

A good place to conduct research is in a bookstore. Look at books in your subject area, and ask yourself which one you would buy. Is it eye-catching? Readable? Well organized? Graphically appealing? If you are self-publishing, work with a graphic artist to achieve that look. If you are submitting the proposal to a publisher, indicate your preferences. Though **Production Details** appear at this point in the proposal, they sometimes can't be finalized until the book is at the production/publishing stage. Remember that you will not always fill in sections of the proposal in the order they appear.

About promotion

This is an important section of your proposal. It will help you and a conventional publisher do the following:
- Assess your willingness, enthusiasm, and cooperation in promoting your book.
- Evaluate your connections and, therefore, how many sales you might generate.
- Provide the promotion department with ideas on how best to reach the market for your book.

This is the way your **About Promotion** section should be organized. The lead should be enthusiastic and convincing. It should indicate your willingness to help promote your book and lay out a plan for doing so: "I will work closely

< 33 >

with the sales and publicity team of the publisher to…" or "I am committed to promoting my book by doing the following…"

The body should include all the ways in which you plan to promote your book. Here are some examples:

- Present lectures and workshops
- Send out press releases and review copies prior to publication
- Write magazine articles
- Arrange for book reviews
- Do book signings
- Appear on radio or TV talk shows
- Delineate media (websites, local newspapers, special-interest publications, event calendars, book-review sections, radio, TV)

The conclusion should be punchy and enthusiastic and demonstrate your belief in your book and willingness to go for it.

Table of contents

One way to build your table of contents is with a technique called a mind map, which looks like a wheel. The center of the map is the subject of the book. Each of the spokes is a subject area that may turn into a chapter. For now, it is enough just to think about all the areas you want to cover in relation to the subject of your book. Write a main topic on each line. There will be as many spokes as there are topics. Later, you may combine some and eliminate others.

< 34 >

The next step is to fill in key points under each subject area. Eventually, these will be the subheads in your chapters. When you add these to your mind map, it will look something like a windmill. If you prefer outlining to mind-mapping, the principle is the same. Your main subject areas are Roman numerals, and the key points become A, B, C, and so on. Another way to think of an outline is to consider it as the skeleton of your book. As you add information under each key point, you are building your chapters, one section at a time.

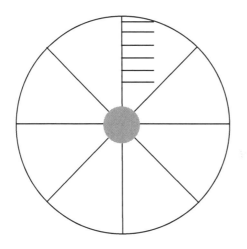

Once you have mind-mapped your main subject areas and the key points under each subject, you are ready to turn those headings into chapter titles. They are working titles for now and can be refined later. One of the most important elements of the proposal is your **Table of Contents,** which is your content in a nutshell, but there is more to the **Table of Contents** than chapter headings. A book consists of

< 35 >

three parts—front matter, chapters, and back matter—and the **Table of Contents** must reflect all three. (Front and Back Matter are discussed in detail in the section on **Writing** on page 41).

Dedication
Acknowledgments
Foreword
Preface
Introduction
Chapter 1
Chapter 2
Chapter 3
Chapter 4
Chapter 5
Chapter 6
Chapter 7
Chapter 8
Epilogue
Appendix
Glossary
Index

Chapter summaries

Each chapter summary is the way you envision the finished chapter. It contains the chapter's rationale, process, and key points. A paragraph is sufficient. A summary is the heart of what will become a full-blown chapter. It forces you to explain what the chapter will cover and how it will be

< 36 >

organized. If you have done the necessary research and thought through your content, your chapter summaries will be clear and concise.

Sample chapter

This is where the rubber meets the road. The first chapter is the hardest, but once you master the way you want to approach the writing, it becomes a template for the rest. The chapters are the heart of the book and, of course, take the most time. They are the reason you are writing—the cake. All the rest is frosting. Start with Chapter 1, if each chapter is going to build on the one before it, or with your favorite topic if they are not. This is to help you find your voice, pace, and style. If you submit this proposal to a publisher, the chapter you attach to your proposal must provide a sample of your best writing and of the caliber of your book.

Putting the Proposal in Proper Order

Now, you are going to fill in the most important parts of the proposal: your **Concept Statement** and **About the Book.** You can only do that after you have completed all the other sections. In the actual proposal, they go at the beginning.

Concept statement (This appears first in the proposal but is written last.)

The Concept Statement must grab the reader's attention and make that person want to read the rest of the document. The reader could be an editor, a potential publisher, or an agent. This is your billboard, so your message has to be con-

< 37 >

cise, powerful, and enticing. It is usually only a few paragraphs long and should do the following:

- Clarify the purpose and subject matter of the book.
- Demonstrate how the book differs from others on the market.
- Explain why this is the right book at the right time.
- Describe the book's greatest benefit and how that benefit is delivered.
- Identify the target audience.
- Summarize the author's credentials.
- Generate enthusiasm with an upbeat tone, active verbs, persuasive language, and powerful descriptions.

Summarize main points in *your* concept statement in no more than two or three paragraphs.

About the book

This appears as the first major section of your proposal (after the **Concept Statement** and **Proposal Contents**) and encapsulates all the sections that follow. It is very important, since, if it doesn't meet the acquisition editor's needs, he or she may not read any further. That is the reason you are filling it out *after* you have done as much of the proposal as possible. There are two ways to handle **About the Book.** One is to begin with the big picture and narrow the topic with supporting details; the other is to begin with specifics and expand to the broader context.

< 38 >

Big picture first

1. The social, political, or cultural context
2. Why this is the right time for this book
3. The problem for which the book will offer a solution
4. Any testimonials
5. Strengths and weaknesses of existing books
6. The book's strongest features and greatest benefit
7. Lists, statistics, authoritative quotes to underscore unique features
8. Author's credentials
9. Audience, market
10. How market will be reached, promotion suggestions
11. An upbeat conclusion that emphasizes the most unique contribution of your book, its timeliness, its marketability

Book first

To put the book first and big picture last simply invert this list. Sell the book; then, gradually demonstrate what problem it will solve and why this is the time to publish it.

Filling in the blanks

Reading about a proposal is quite different from actually *writing* one. In previous editions of this book, I have left room to fill in the blanks under each heading, but even that is not the same as putting together a proposal step by step.

If you would like a fill-in-the-blank template at no charge, simply go to http://www.writeanonfictionbook.com/Proposal Template.doc. To see two examples of finished proposals,

< 39 >

go to http://www.writeanonfictionbook.com/Proposal_Going-Solo.pdf and http://www.writeanonfictionbook.com/Proposal_AmazingJourney.pdf.

How the Proposal and the Book Overlap

Think of the proposal as the foundation and the book as the house you build on that foundation. Each has its own structure, but the structures are very closely related. Almost every section of the proposal becomes part of the book as content or description on the book jacket or covers. A solid foundation ensures a well-crafted book.

PROPOSAL STRUCTURE	BOOK STRUCTURE
Concept	Front & Back Covers
About the Book	Copyright page
About the Author	Preface
About the Market	Acknowledgements
About the Competition	Introduction
Production Details	Table of Contents
About Promotion	Chapters
Table of Contents	Appendices
Chapter Summaries	Glossary
Sample Chapter	Index

< 40 >

3

STEP 2: WRITING

With your proposal as complete as you can make it at this point, you are ready to start the writing process. In fact, if you've completed your sample chapter, you have already begun. You're probably thinking, it's about time! Believe me, your success in the writing phase is directly proportional to the work you did in planning. Obviously, writing a book is time-consuming. In fact, it should take three to six months, unless you are writing six to eight hours a day, every day, which few of us are able to do. The bulk of the work is in building the chapters, starting with your outline and the chapter summaries and continuing to flesh out the content. That is a very simplistic way of describing the work of writing, but sometimes, simple is best.

The work you have done so far has a dual purpose: to help you think through every aspect of your book and to

< 41 >

provide material you will use in the book. Some of it translates directly, such as the **Table of Contents**; some of it fits into other sections, such as the book covers, the introduction, and the preface. None of it is wasted effort.

The process, beginning on page 15, outlined the steps in all three phases. What follows is a more detailed look at the book's content.

If the book is a hardback, it will have a book jacket; if it is a softcover, the cover will contain the same information as a jacket. The front cover has the title, your name, an illustration, and perhaps an endorsement or quote from a favorable review. The back cover is your full-page ad. It should include a description of the main features of the book, a category, a brief bio and a photo of the author, the publisher, an ISBN, a bar code, and the price. Much of this will already exist in the proposal and can easily be converted to the appropriate language.

Front Matter

Copyright page. This page is usually provided by the publisher, whether that publisher is a conventional one, a print-on-demand (POD) house, or you. It contains certain basic information, such as the title, the author's name, the copyright date, a paragraph explaining copyright rules, the country in which the book is printed, the ISBN, a Library of Congress number, the publisher, its location, and contact information.

Foreword. This should be written by someone other than the author and is particularly powerful when an expert

< 42 >

in the field writes it. If the writer is a person with a recognized name or title, you might want to mention "Foreword by name" on the cover. Sometimes, it is helpful to write the foreword yourself to demonstrate to the expert what you would like to see.

Introduction. Think of the introduction as a practical guide to using the book. It should explain what the book is about, why it was written, and how it should be read, if there is more than one way. If you are expressing a point of view that will enhance the reader's understanding, include it in the introduction. If the story behind the story is interesting, by all means include that as well. This is your chance to explain your rationale.

Preface. This is written by the author and explains why and how you wrote the book. It can tell your story in a very personal way, if you wish.

Acknowledgments. Few of us write our books without help, no matter how well versed we are on the subject matter. There are hundreds of ways in which assistance is given, from people willing to share their expertise and knowledge to editors who turn our rough prose into pearls. Friends or professionals transcribe interviews, proofread manuscripts, listen to us read aloud, and encourage us when we feel we have become brain-dead. If you usually skip over the acknowledgments section in the books you read, I would suggest that you stop and read them. Those who help deserve to be recognized, and some of these sections are wonderful to read.

< 43 >

The Chapters

Of course, the bulk of the writing takes place between the front and back matter. By now, you have mapped out your main headings, which become your table of contents; the key points under each heading; and the one-paragraph chapter summaries. The question is, how do you get from a paragraph to a chapter? Each key point becomes a subhead of your chapter. A summary is the big picture; the subheads are the way you will organize the material. This is the time to fill in the meat—your research, narrative, quotes from interviewees, resource materials, and graphics. The important thing is to get all the pertinent information under each subhead. Later, you can refine the writing and build your transitions.

Back Matter

Bibliography. If you have read other books and quoted other authors, a bibliography acknowledges the sources. Of course, you should attribute quotes in the copy or with footnotes. In some cases, you will have to get written permission to use other people's work and may even have to pay for the privilege. A bibliography also gives readers a list of references to read if they wish to dig more deeply into the subject.

Appendices. Sometimes, you have so much background information or detail that if you included all of it in the main body of work, you might overwhelm your reader. That's what appendices are for. They are a good place to put scientific data, charts, reports, and detailed explanations without ruining the flow of your text.

< 44 >

Glossary. This is an optional, alphabetically arranged dictionary of terms peculiar to the subject of the book. Try to define such words in the text.

Epilogue. If you have "one last thought," this is the place to express it.

Index. When a book is filled with facts or topics a reader might want to find quickly, an index is the fastest way to find them. There are two types of indexes—subject-matter and detailed. I strongly suggest you hire a professional indexer instead of using the index feature of your word-processing program.

Building a Book

Building a book is like building anything else: You begin with the basics, and you add one element at a time. The most important content is in the middle—the chapters. Logically, you should write those first. What goes in the introduction, for example, depends on how the book is organized, as well as several other factors. You can't write the index until you have finished the book. Remember, you don't have to write the whole book in one sitting, nor should you. Ultimately, writing is a do-it-yourself process. No matter how much support or help you have, when you sit down at the computer, it comes down to you and the words.

Research

Wonderful as it would be to just let the words pour forth, before we write, most of us have to gather information. Usually, that takes a sizeable chunk of time, even when we know

< 45 >

our subject. When I look back on the books I've written, I can only think of two for which I did just sit down and write, and both were on writing. The first was *Going Solo: How to Survive & Thrive as a Freelance Writer*; the second, *Words To Live By: Reflections on the writing life from a 40-year veteran*. I knew the subject matter because I had lived it.

Other books have required much more research. Besides interviews, I surfed the Web and printed out reams of information (much of which turned out to be irrelevant, self-serving, or just plain worthless); bought, read, and high-lighted books on my subject; listened to audiotapes; and absorbed any and all information I could amass. Frequently, as I found myself revisiting the same topics over and over again, I reread my own books and old notes. I thought of it as recycling. In other words, research is looking for the kind of information you need to write your book. So, where should you look? I would suggest seven sources:

1. Interviews

The first rule of interviewing is **find an expert.** For most of my career, this has been my starting point. There is no better source than an expert and no more direct and understand-able way to learn about a subject than to listen to someone talk about something he or she loves. When I first began writing feature articles on a wide variety of topics, I tried to find one person who had the patience of a saint, the ability to explain the essence of the subject, and the contacts to direct me to others who would do the same.

< 46 >

Rule two is **use every listening skill at your disposal.** If you don't understand what you're hearing, ask for clarification. You are there to learn, not to show the other person how much you know. After each question, summarize, in your own words, what you understood; then, build your next question on that point. In my mind, an interview is a conversation, a dialogue, with the primary speaker being the interviewee. Simply put, *this conversation is not about you;* it's about the other person and what that person is willing to share with you.

The third rule is **continue to build your understanding and knowledge base** with every question and with every person you talk to. Use what you learned in the first interview as the basis for the second and so on. You may feel like a lost soul with the first expert, a little more informed with the second; but by the time you get to the third, you will finally be involved in a meaningful dialogue. That's when you know you are doing it right.

2. Research room of the public library

Your best friend should be the research librarian at your local library. Before everything was computerized, librarians acted essentially as walking databases for every possible source of information. If you asked them how you could find information on a particular subject, they could point you to the area of the room, the shelf, and the precise reference book you needed. They still do that, of course, but their scope is even broader now due to the numerous specialized websites they can access at the touch of a finger. I am con-

< 47 >

vinced that reference librarians are wizards, and their computers are imbued with magic.

I was going to list essential books for writers, such as Bowker's *Books in Print*, stylebooks, almanacs, and desk references, but the research librarian (my best friend) informed me that 90 percent of research is done through their full-text databases, which can be accessed from home or branch libraries.

3. University and specialized libraries

These are little-known sources of valuable information. If you haven't visited one, do it just for your general education, if not for a specific subject. Most universities have a large central library and several special-collection libraries, such as Art and Architecture, Business, Earth and Planetary Sciences, Law, Medicine, Music, and Social Work.

4. Books on your subject area

There is no such thing as a new idea. Believe me, if you've thought of it, someone else has too, and that person has probably written a book about it. That doesn't mean you should abandon your idea; it simply means another author has tackled it in a different way than you will. How do you find all of these other books? From three sources:

- Bookstores with large selections. Ask someone at the customer service desk for the section on your subject. Then, make yourself at home with a pen and pad or a laptop computer. The biggest bookstore in the world is amazon. com. Just search for your topic and you will find a long list of titles.

< 48 >

- Public library. If you have a list of topics, ask the librarian how to find them, or type the topic into the computer. If you don't have a list, just ask for one.
- Online. Start with amazon.com, bn.com, half.com, and fearlessbooks.com/Indies.html. This is a fast way to find titles, synopses, and reviews; for many researchers, it is sufficient. I personally like the feel of books in my hands. If you want the real book, this is one way to find out about it.

5. *Corporations*

Want to know about a specific industry or publicly held company within that industry? Start collecting annual reports. If you are a shareholder, you should have one or can easily secure one from your stockbroker or directly from the company. If you're not, sometimes you can simply call the company's public relations department and ask for one. If you're not a shareholder but have a stockbroker or know one, request annual reports through the brokerage firms. Check the public libraries to see whether they maintain a file of annual reports.

The next sources are magazine and newspaper articles about industries and companies. Start with the computer in the reference room of the library to find them, either in the stacks or on CD-ROM. (The days of microfilm are gone, by and large, and we are all grateful for that!) Business publications, such as *The Wall Street Journal, Business Week, Forbes, Fortune,* and *Barron's,* are rich sources of information as well.

< 49 >

6. Government agencies

There is so much literature put out by federal government agencies, it boggles the mind. (I printed out a thirty-two-page, single-spaced list of agency names from http://www.lib.lsu.edu/gov/tree.) It is there for the asking, and much of it is free of charge. What follows are the major categories listed on the website. Under each category are all the sub-sections, offices, and assistant secretaries. It is a treasure trove for anyone willing to search through the links.

- Boards, commissions, and committees
- Foundations
- Executive agencies
- Marketing and regulatory programs
- Natural resources and environment
- Research, education, and economics
- Rural development
- National Telecommunications and Information Administration
- Patent and Trademark Office
- Technology Administration
- National Technical Information Service (NTIS)
- Departments of Agriculture, Commerce, Defense, Education, Energy, Health and Human Services, Homeland Security, Housing and Urban Development, Justice, Labor, State, Transportation, Veterans Affairs, Interior, and Treasury
- Food and Drug Administration
- National Institutes of Health

< 50 >

- Independent administrations, agencies, boards, commissions, corporations, and services
- Judicial
- Legislative
- Library of Congress

7. The Internet

Depending on your generation, this is going to be your first thought or your last; either way, it is your most important source of information. The secret of researching on the World Wide Web is knowing how to use search engines. It is a science that assumes you think like a computer, which most of us do not. Every search engine has a place to go for helpful hints on how to use it most effectively. Since the first edition of this book, Google has not only become the undisputed king of search engines, it is now a verb. If you want to find something, "Google it."

Time to Write

If you go to any bookstore and look in the writing section, you may be amazed by the sheer number of choices. There seems to be a book on every genre you might ever have thought of attempting, from romances to mysteries, from poetry to screenplays. At the very least, you can immediately eliminate those four categories, since you are writing a nonfiction book.

But, even at that, your book might be historical, reportorial, self-help, or humorous; it might be a memoir, personal philosophy, or commentary. Each will require a special

< 51 >

technique, and I encourage you to read anything you can find that will help you perfect your personal style. What I want to talk about here is the *process* of writing—how to get started and how to keep the momentum going once you have gotten your first paragraph on paper.

The good news is that if you have gone through the steps in planning, you have already begun. Your basic outline, including main headings and key points, is complete. Ideally, you have also written your chapter summaries and sample chapter. If so, you're on your way.

If not, you still have a couple of hurdles to overcome. The biggest hurdle is actually believing you can write. It may amaze you that you decided to write a book, worked your way through the proposal process, thought you were ready to write, and suddenly found your fingers frozen to the computer keys. What happened?

Explanations I've heard:

- I'm a speaker, not a writer. This is an entirely different discipline.
- When I teach it, everyone says I make the subject clear and easy to understand. When I write, unfortunately, it comes out sounding like a law book.
- What I've learned from this process is that I don't really want to write a book.
- When I try to convey what I know, I get completely blocked.

< 52 >

Observations from teaching and coaching:

- Writing seems so mysterious to many people that they are afraid to try.
- Sometimes, when they do the research for a proposal, potential authors discover there is no market for their books or even enough substance to justify writing them.
- When they do get two or three sentences down on paper or the computer screen, non-writers are often uncertain about grammar and punctuation.
- Despite having a solid outline to work from, many first-time authors don't know where to go from there.

Suggestions based on the preceding statements:

If you are more comfortable speaking or teaching and you can't translate what you say into the written word, try recording your presentations or dictating your thoughts into a digital recorder, Dragon Naturally Speaking for PCs, or Mac-Speech Dictate for Macs. You'll find that your "voice" comes through loud and clear.

If you have discovered through your research process that you don't really have the book you thought you had, there is already something out there that does the same job as well or better, or there simply is no market for your book, you are fortunate. It is better to discover it now than later. That's exactly what planning is all about.

Writing a book is hard work, even for people who have done it before. Perhaps you have learned through this process

< 53 >

that you really don't want to invest yourself. Why write a book when you know you have no desire to do it? I can't think of one good reason.

If you haven't written, you don't know if you're any good at it. This isn't school, so no one is grading your paper. It's just you and the blank computer screen. You have nothing to lose by sitting down and expressing your thoughts. You may like what you've written; you may not. But at least you have begun, and that's the hardest part.

If you don't think grammar, spelling, and punctuation are your strong suits, help is available. See the **Recommended Reading** section of this book beginning on page 159 for some of the best grammar books in print; use spell check (don't count on it, though) and your dictionary; take a course; or hire an editor and a copy editor (see **Professional Partners** on page 85 for how these two editors differ).

Rules to Live By

- **Don't talk about writing.** Don't explain your story or your article or your book until your listeners are bleary-eyed. If you have something to say, write it. Writing is not something you discuss; it is something you do. The only thing you can say out loud is, "My book is about..." and finish the sentence.
- **Know your subject.** Most things require research. Don't skimp on this step. In fact, overdo it if possible. You'll never know everything there is to know about any topic. The more information you have, the better you can

< 54 >

explain it clearly, concisely, and very carefully. If you have ten pages of data, you should be able to compress them into a few really tight paragraphs. If you can't, you didn't understand the material.

- **Take time to process what you have learned.** Your subconscious mind is a computer. Everything you feed into it is churning around in there—organizing itself, coming to conclusions, solving problems, getting ready to bring forth a finished product. All you have to do is translate it into the right words. When I first stumbled on this principle in a book called *Psycho-Cybernetics* by Maxwell Maltz, computers filled rooms and the PC was a distant dream. Maltz referred to them as servo-mechanism machines. That was a mouthful, but the man was ahead of his time.

- **Have respect for words.** Learn a lot of them. If you don't know what they mean, look them up. Don't use the same word twice. Find the perfect synonym. Buy the best dictionary (*Webster's New World College Dictionary*) and thesaurus (*Oxford American Writer's Thesaurus*). Compare what you find to online sources. I grew up with books, so I reach for them first, but there are great tools on the Internet. Look for them and use them. Don't trust spell-check. It will often give you the wrong word—*there* when you mean *they're*, *it's* when you want *its*, *apiece* when you typed *a piece*.

- **Grammar counts**. Nothing—absolutely nothing—is worse than a piece of writing filled with inexcusable errors. Of course, you will need an editor at some point; but if you

< 55 >

can't construct a decent sentence with proper punctuation, take a course, buy a book (*Chicago Manual of Style*, 16th Edition), hire a tutor. Grammar and punctuation are the foundation of everything you write. Start there and build.

• **Finally, trust your gut.** When your writing is mechanical, awkward, overly wordy, sloppy, or unclear, you'll know it. Don't muscle your way through a bad sentence. Don't keep something because it's "beautiful" and you love the sound of it; but it doesn't fit, doesn't say anything, and doesn't advance your story. It's hard, I know, but highlight the whole thing and hit the delete button. Your "Jury of the Deep" (inner voices, for you who don't know me) is never wrong. Never.

How to Organize Your Files

I was commiserating with a friend about how hard it is to keep all the research and drafts organized when you are writing a book. "You should see my office," I confided, as I took in the files and piles associated with my latest project. "Oh, I know," she said. "My stuff is all over my table, the island in the middle of my kitchen, and all the steps leading down to my den. I can hardly walk around this room." I formed a mental picture of her kitchen and suddenly felt better.

"If I had to find something in this mess," my friend confided, "I'd be in big trouble." I couldn't second that thought because I was certain I would be able to find any piece of paper I needed in less than a minute—if not the piece of

< 56 >

paper itself, then definitely the exact place I had filed it.

It occurred to me, after I finished the phone conversation, that I had never seen a chapter in any book for writers on how to organize the mountain of notes, articles, interviews, and assorted other materials that accumulate in the process of researching and writing a book. (That doesn't mean there isn't such a chapter, only that I have never seen one.)

When you are writing something as complex as a book, you will accumulate a lot of "stuff." If you don't have a system for keeping it all together, you will go stark raving mad before you get to Chapter 3.

I have always had a system, but I can't remember whether it came about intuitively or by trial and error. In any event, it works, and I am happy to share it.

1. There are two parts to any filing system for your book: paper and electronic. That means for every tangible paper file folder, you should have a corresponding folder on your computer hard drive. Everything that goes in your electronic files should have a duplicate in your paper files.
2. The kind of file folder you use is a matter of personal preference. Because chapters tend to expand and files take a lot of punishment, I like sturdy classification folders with at least two dividers and places to attach several sets of two-hole-punched papers.

Setting Up the Filing System

1. Create a folder on your computer with the title or nickname of your book. Inside that folder, create a folder for

< 57 >

each chapter. Label them with the chapters' nicknames or, for simplicity's sake, Chapter 1, 2, 3, etc. Then label a set of cardboard folders exactly the same way. Keep the headings simple because the point is to remember them easily.

2. Whatever you put in your electronic files should have a duplicate in your paper files. For example, if you download something from the Internet that applies to a particular chapter, save it to that chapter's folder and, unless it's huge, print out a copy for your paper files. Save anything you write for any of the chapters to the proper folder, and put a hard copy in the corresponding paper folder.

3. The only exception to that rule would be if you have printed material with no corresponding computer file, and chances are you will accumulate quite a bit of paper as you do your research.

4. Did I mention books? I always seem to refer to books I already own, buy for a particular project, or take out of the library. Where do they go? Preferably, all in one place—on the desk, under the desk, or in a conveniently located bookcase. The idea is to be able to get to them when you need them and remember where you put them when you don't.

5. Of course, save your work often, and ALWAYS back up all your files to another hard drive or a flash drive.

Chances are you will end up with all sorts of things that don't fit neatly into existing categories, which are your

< 58 >

chapters. Then what? More file folders. Besides my chapter files, on my desk or under it, are folders labeled with everything else. Most of those are full of printed material, but in some cases there are also electronic files, which are filed in duplicate folders inside the book folder on my hard drive.

Is this complicated? Not really. So what's the big deal?

1. Well, first, unless you are an extremely organized person or an experienced writer who has done this for past projects, you may not have given any thought to setting up a dual filing system.
2. Second, this whole process should take place the minute you decide on your main subject areas or table of contents and before you begin any other aspect of your book.
3. And, finally, every piece of information you handle—electronic or paper—should be filed in its proper folder, on the computer and in hard-copy form if possible, as soon as you are finished with it.

I know this is a lot of work, but it's worth it for two reasons: (1) You will always be able to put your hands on anything you want in less than a minute; and (2) whatever room you work in, you can confine everything related to your book to a very manageable space.

How to save your files

There is one more step to a perfect book-filing system: the way you save documents within all those file folders. Imagine you are writing a book on communication, and one of

< 59 >

the chapters is on meetings. Within your main folder—**Book Files** or **Communication**—is a folder called **Chapter 1: Meetings.** Within that file folder is a document titled "Meetings," draft #1, and the date you wrote it. This is how to save the document:

Meetings_1_04111

Now, let's say you are going to make changes to that document, but you don't want to lose your original version. Before you write a single word, save it as Meetings_2_051111. Then, make your changes to the new draft. When you are finished, save the latest version. Within your **Meetings** folder your now have two files:

Meetings_1_04111

Meetings_2_051111

If you are doing a lot of rewriting, you may accumulate numerous drafts of each chapter. In the case of ten drafts, for example, your **Meetings** file folder would look like this:

Meetings 1_041111

Meetings 2_051111

Meetings 3_052011

Meetings 4_052511

Meetings 5_062511

Meetings 6_070211

Meetings 7_071111

Meetings 8_071211

Meetings 9_071611

Meetings10_072011

Why bother going to all this trouble? You never know when you are going to want to refer to or use something

< 60 >

you've written weeks or even months ago. If you had simply typed over your original words, they would be gone forever. Don't imagine you will be able to remember what you wrote; after ten drafts of one chapter, believe me, you won't. When the book is finished and in print, you can throw away your old drafts if you want to.

Writing Guidelines

You have done all the getting ready anyone could possibly do. Now it's time to write. This is the one area for which there is no list of instructions. I've been writing more than half my life and, as I look back, I don't remember anyone actually telling me what to do or how to do it. I made a lot of mistakes until I got the feel of my own rhythm and style, but eventually it became as natural as flipping the switch on my little Smith Corona electric, portable typewriter and putting my fingers on the keys. By the time I wrote my first little book, I had been a feature writer for many years, and it wasn't much of a stretch to think of a book as a very long article. The rules were pretty much the same; it just had more content and took longer. The following guidelines have served me well as an author:

Guideline 1: *Do not make your first book your first experience with writing.* That would be like going from grammar school to graduate school. You need to be comfortable with the writing process before you tackle a book. Even after many years of writing for a living, when I started my first book, I felt like a stranger in a strange land.

< 61 >

Guideline 2: *Learn to type, and increase your speed and accuracy. You will never be sorry.* Way back, in the beginning of my career, I could sit at that little typewriter at my desk for many uninterrupted hours, lost in space as my fingers pounded on the keys. I wasn't a good typist then, and I have not improved a lot, unfortunately. It has made for a lot of retyping and spell-checking, just to get the words unscrambled.

Guideline 3: *Have a plan and a set of deadlines. When it's time to write (you know what's coming), write.* I freelanced for more than four years before I became a full-time writer. In the meantime, I worked, ran a house, had kids, and chased a dog around. But when it was time to write, I wrote, no matter what time it was. When I had deadlines as a staff writer, when it was time to write, I wrote, whether I was in the mood or not. When I started writing books, I did it "in my spare time," after I had sometimes written all day. Again, when it was time to write, I wrote, even if I would have preferred to be sleeping.

Guideline 4: *Be scrupulously honest with yourself. If you get that little pang of doubt, go with it.* At first, it's like a tiny inner voice whispering, yuck. Later, if you're lucky, it gets louder. The point is, when it doesn't feel right, you know it. Don't con yourself that it's OK. It's not. And don't fall in love with your own pearls on paper. On the other hand, don't polish until you take all the luster off the page. Know when to

< 62 >

stop editing. There are two ways to go about this: (1) Just let it pour and fix it later; or (2) write a little, fix it; write a little more, fix it; and so forth. I've done it both ways. Sometimes, it is just flowing, and there's no stopping the words. Other times, I have to polish every sentence until I just about drive myself crazy. But I do have one lucky gift: the innate sense of when something is just plain wrong. I reread a sentence; I know instantly whether it's forced or awkward or wordy or phony, and I hit the delete key. When there are too many sentences like that, what I call a rock slide, I get up and walk away.

Guideline 5: *Don't hurry. Figure out how much time you need with gaps in between and plan accordingly.* Writing can't be rushed. You're not trying to make the early edition; you're writing a book, perhaps your first. Between writing times, do something other than think about the book. I've always been a believer in leaving space between work sessions. I take a day to review research and then sleep on it. I write, reread, leave it alone, and sleep on it. The next day, the creative juices flow, the information has rearranged itself, and I can spot bad writing I missed the day before.

Guideline 6: *Take care of your health. Eat well; sleep as much as you need to; stretch frequently; exercise.* This is work you're doing. A little training will go a long way. After a day of writing, I'm pretty much good for nothing. My energy, especially mental energy, is depleted; my eyes burn;

< 63 >

my shoulders are in knots; and I'm just plain tired. Writing an article may be a sprint, but writing a book is a marathon.

Guideline 7: *Give yourself a well-deserved pat on the back for a job well done.* You set a challenge for yourself—sometimes only a few pages, sometimes, more—and you met it. You have done what you set out to do. You have worked on your book, and you should be very proud of yourself. If you haven't yet gotten the hang of self-congratulations, allow me to be the first to tell you how great you are! When I'm through writing something big, like a book, I tend to feel a sense of letdown. It's the process of writing I love, though I know not everyone does. I'm happier writing than having written, but I am learning to enjoy the valleys and accept the kudos when it comes. For many writers, this is hard to do because so much of our identity comes from what we do. The binders full of samples and the shelf of books with my name on their spines are great, but I've had to learn to appreciate them as much as doing what it took to make them a reality.

Writing Your Outline

The most important step in the planning process is writing your outline. Let's start with the main points, which you have already mapped out on page 34 of this book. Here is an example from one of my books, *Shoptalk: 6 ways to get your message across at work.*

I.   Are you listening?

II. What you say and how you say it

< 64 >

III. The art and craft of writing
IV. The telephone: friend or foe?
V. Speaking without words
VI. Meetings: the living laboratory

Now let's break it down and add subheads under each main point:

I. Are you listening?
    A. The art of listening
    B. A listening attitude
    C. The right questions

II. What you say and how you say it
    A. Physical and psychological aspects
    B. The obstacle course
    C. Small talk
    D. Presentations

III. The art and craft of writing
    A. Why bother?
    B. Look it up
    C. Letters, letters, letters
    D. Back to basics

Now, you are going to build the book by plugging in any research you have or points you want to make—right into the outline. I will warn you that this can be a very untidy process for a while. If you think of each subheading as a file folder and each piece of information as something you are

< 65 >

filing, just drop it in. You can always clean it up later. Right now, the point is to keep adding material. Here is what that might look like in its very early stages:

I. Are You Listening?

   A. The art of listening: Why don't we listen well?

      1. We hear what we expect to hear and ignore everything else.

      2. We filter through our own experience and perceptions.

      3. Words mean different things to different people.

      4. We feel an urgency to express our thoughts and feelings.

   B. A listening attitude

      1. Sincerely attend to what the other person is saying.

      2. Try to understand the meaning and intent of words.

      3. Give the speaker your full attention.

      4. Try to care about what is being said; concentrate.

      5. E.A.R.

         E = enthusiasm for listening

         A = attention to the speaker

         R = reinforcement by feedback

   C. The right questions

      1. Good questions are the most powerful communication tool.

      2. Good questions demonstrate your intelligence and your attention.

      3. People love questions so they can talk.

      4. Questions do these things: persuade … gather

< 66 >

information … plant ideas … clear up fuzzy thinking … defuse volatile situations … clarify instructions … reduce anxiety … overcome objections … solve problems … motivate people.

Chapter summaries

When you have enough information to visualize your chapter, write one or two paragraphs that include your main headings and key points. For the chapter on listening, it might look like this:

If any ability is underrated and neglected, it is certainly that of listening and truly hearing what is said. Yet, listening should be the first and most important communication skill on your list—especially in your job. Since you are usually the principal link between an outside person and your boss, you act as a conveyor of all kinds of messages. If you don't hear something and understand it completely, that's as good as guaranteeing it will be lost in translation.

Your writing plan

Writing a book, even a small one, takes time. The first two questions are how much time do you have, and how are you going to allocate it? This is the point at which you may feel more than a little overwhelmed by the task ahead. Take a few deep breaths—inhale, exhale, inhale, exhale. No kidding. Do it. Inhale, exhale. OK, now sit down and make a list of everything you have to write, which you will find on pages 17-18 of this book.

< 67 >

For the front and back covers, you will need your title and subtitle, a brief descriptive paragraph about the book, your bio, and a couple of powerful endorsements, which you won't have until the book is written. Skip the copyright page for now. The publisher or you will supply it later. You will write the preface, introduction, acknowledgments, index, bibliography, and appendices after you finish the heart of the book. I have covered in some detail how to build each chapter. Now write down these dates:

Deadlines

Today's date _____

Deadline for first draft of all chapters _____

Deadline for second draft of all chapters _____

Deadline for third draft of all chapters _____

Deadline for preface _____

Deadline for introduction _____

Deadline for acknowledgments _____

Deadline for second draft of front matter _____

Deadline for references _____

Deadline for bibliography _____

Deadline for appendices _____

Deadline for index _____

Deadline for any other back matter _____

Deadline for second draft of back matter _____

Deadline for copy-edited manuscript _____

Deadline for revisions of copy-editing _____

Deadline for final draft of book _____

Deadline for graphic designer _____

< 68 >

Deadline for proofreading layout _____
Dropdead deadline for printer _____

The deadlines may be those you set for yourself or those set for you by a publisher. In either case, they are sacrosanct.

The time between today's date and when you plan to send the finished layout to the printer or publisher is all the time you have. Everything on the list must fit in that time frame. You already know that the bulk of your writing time will be taken up by the chapters, which are the heart of the book. But the preface and introduction are every bit as important. Remember, the first is personal, and the second is informative. Be sure to give each the proper tone.

Starting from the deadline for the first draft, work backward to determine exactly how much time you have, what has to be done, and how long each segment will take. Set mini-deadlines for yourself for each segment, and block them out on a large calendar. Be realistic. If it can't be done in the time allotted, something has to be changed, and it may be your deadline. If you are self-publishing, you can move your own deadlines; if you are working with a conventional publisher, deadlines can be negotiated. When they are impossible, you have a right to say so, *before* you sign the contract.

< 69 >

How to Organize Your Files

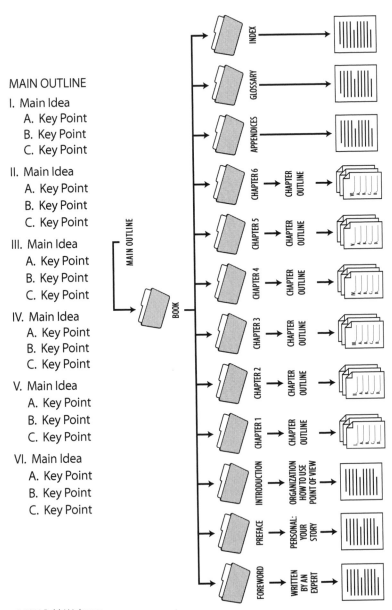

MAIN OUTLINE

I. Main Idea
   A. Key Point
   B. Key Point
   C. Key Point

II. Main Idea
   A. Key Point
   B. Key Point
   C. Key Point

III. Main Idea
   A. Key Point
   B. Key Point
   C. Key Point

IV. Main Idea
   A. Key Point
   B. Key Point
   C. Key Point

V. Main Idea
   A. Key Point
   B. Key Point
   C. Key Point

VI. Main Idea
   A. Key Point
   B. Key Point
   C. Key Point

© 2011 Bobbi Linkemer

< 70 >

Writing Details

1. **How, when, and where:** Do you prefer to write on a legal pad or at a computer? In total silence or with music or the radio in the background? At a coffee shop or curled up in bed? At the crack of dawn or in the middle of the night? Whatever your personal style, if it has been working for you, don't abandon it because you think there is a "right way to write." The only right way is your way.

2. **Time and perspective:** Where, how, and at what time of the day or night you write is one part of your approach. A second part is the perspective, or person, you choose for your book. If you are writing as yourself, using the pronoun *I*, you are writing in first person. When you speak to your reader, using the pronoun *you*, it is called second person. If you are writing about your subject as an observer or a narrator—using pronouns like *he*, *she*, *his*, *hers*, *they*, and *theirs*—it's called third person. Whatever you decide, don't switch midstream unless it will make sense to the reader.

3. **Tense:** Does your book take place in the present, past, or future? When you quote someone, do you attribute the quote with the word "say" or "said"? This may seem a bit simplistic, but the point here is consistency. Person and tense cannot roam all over the place. You may have to experiment a bit before you decide which way to go, but once you do decide, stick with one tense. You will probably slip from time to time (we all do), but that's why you hire (or the publisher hires) a copy editor. (More on this under **Professional Partners** on page 89)

< 71 >

4. **Style:** This refers to the very special way you write—the familiar, recognizable feel of the writing. You may not discover your voice immediately. The key to voice is allowing yourself to be natural and unforced. That, of course, takes self-confidence. If you are a relatively new author, you may still be developing your confidence, but believe me, it will come.

Think of it this way: If your spoken voice is your distinctive sound, your writer's voice is your singular written style. This is particularly important for nonfiction writers. When people read something you have written—a book, an article, an essay, or a letter—they will recognize it as yours.

Finding Your Voice

1. **Be real, natural.** If possible, write the way you speak, even if the grammar is a little shaky at first.
2. **Start a conversation with your readers.** Connect with them; engage them; answer their potential questions.
3. **Concentrate on content, not style.** What you say is more important than how you say it. You can't cover up lack of knowledge with words, words, and more words.
4. **Think with your fingers.** Put them on the keys, and keep them there. Let the thoughts pour out, even if they seem jumbled.
5. **Avoid jargon.** Business, technical, political, academic, medical, any kind. Jargon is like speaking in code; it excludes the reader.

< 72 >

6. **Don't change your voice for different audiences.** All you have to be is clear, conversational, and concise. Don't pretend to be a CEO to write to businesspeople or a medical expert to write to doctors. Don't pretend, period.
7. **Don't try too hard.** Some things develop in their own time. Your writer's voice is one of them.

The Legal Side of Writing

Copyright protection is on everyone's mind. It often seems that as we browse a newspaper or turn on the radio, there is another story. From YouTube and file-sharing debates to feature-film pirating, copyright is everywhere.

What is copyright? Copyright is a set of rights that regulates a unique way of presenting an idea or information. At its most basic level, it is really "the right to copy" an original creation. Usually, these rights are for a fixed length of time. The notation for copyright may be written out or typed as either (c), ©, or the word *copyright* spelled out. Copyright may apply to a variety of creative, conceptual, or artistic forms or "works," ranging from poems to plays, photographs to paintings, and dozens of other endeavors. Copyright is one of the laws covered by the greater term "intellectual property."

What is not protected by copyright? Copyright law covers only the precise form or manner in which ideas or information have been produced. It is not designed or intended

< 73 >

to cover the actual ideas, concepts, facts, styles, or techniques that may be represented by the copyrighted product.

How long does copyright last? Copyright lasts for different time periods, depending on the part of the country, the category of work, and whether the work is published or unpublished. In most areas, the duration of copyright for many works is the life of the author plus seventy years.

What happens after copyright expires? In the United States, all books and other items published before 1923 have expired copyrights and are in the public domain, and all works created by the U.S. government, regardless of date, enter the public domain upon their creation. If the author has been dead more than seventy years, the work is most likely in the public domain.

How is copyright transferred? Under the U.S. Copyright Act, if you want to transfer ownership of your copyright, you must do it in writing. No official transfer form is required. A simple document that describes the work involved and the rights being granted is adequate. Non-exclusive grants or licenses need not be in writing under U.S. law. A non-exclusive grant occurs when you allow someone to include a paragraph from your book in his or her work. Your approval can be oral or even implied. Transfers of copyright ownership, including exclusive licenses, should be formally

< 74 >

noted in the U.S. Copyright Office. While filing for copyright is not mandated to make it effective, doing so offers important benefits.

How is copyright obtained? You can download the paperwork yourself from the U.S. Copyright Office at www.copyright.gov/forms. This is the most economic option as the U.S. Copyright Office commonly charges $50 per submission. You will need to select the right form for your work type, but the Copyright Office does a fairly good job of organizing their forms so users can find what they need. Browse through their online help files for assistance on how to fill out the forms and what materials you will need to submit.

How is permission granted to quote a source? Many publishers supply a form to be used when requesting permission to quote from their publications. A typical form calls for the following information:

1. Title of the book to be quoted from
2. Nature of the work in which the selection will be used
3. Name of the author or compiler
4. Publisher of the new work
5. Intended date of publication
6. Selection to be quoted
7. Total pages or total lines
8. Market for which rights are requested (United States and Canada, world in English, or world in all languages)

< 75 >

How should acknowledgments be phrased? Sometimes, the copyright owner permits the borrower to phrase the credit lines and to choose where they will be placed. The borrower can then approximate a uniform style for the acknowledgments and either group them together or place each one in a footnote. When a publisher specifies the phrasing and placement to be used in the credit line, these instructions should be followed precisely.

When and how should footnotes be used?
The first citation of a work, especially if there is not a full bibliography in the book, should contain the following information, in this order:
1. Author's name, as given on the title page
2. Title of the book, including the subtitle (underline or italicize)
3. Edition, if other than the first
4. Title of the series, if significant (do not underline or put in quotation marks)
5. Place of publication (home office)
6. Publisher
7. Date of publication
8. Volume and page numbers

What to Write About
The sky's the limit when it comes to subject matter. There is only one rule: If it's made up, it's fiction; if it's grounded in fact, it's nonfiction. That gives the author a lot of flexibility. It is generally assumed that authors of nonfiction are writing

< 76 >

truthful and accurate accounts of events, but recent scandals have revealed that isn't always the case.

An example was the best-selling memoir *A Million Little Pieces* by James Frey, published in 2003. When it became known that things he had written about as fact never happened, Oprah Winfrey, who had defended him on her show, apparently changed her mind. Frey apologized on national television, but creative nonfiction had already suffered a black eye.

Despite this controversy, memoir remains popular, especially among my students and clients. New authors are often advised to write about what they know and if there is one thing we all know, it is ourselves, or so we would like to believe. *Webster's New World Dictionary* defines a memoir as "a narrative composed from personal experience" or "an autobiography." I think there is a difference between those two genres in both intention and style. An autobiography covers an entire life; a memoir deals with a segment or period of time (teenage years; teaching experience; relationship with a family member).

Ten ways to structure a memoir

1. A theme or a thread
2. Chronological order
3. Flashbacks
4. Function: how things work
5. Journey: circular changes, from beginning to end
6. Mosaic: pieces of a puzzle or little vignettes
7. Organic: physical qualities or layout

< 77 >

8. Origins: how things came to be or are made
9. People or characters
10. The seasons

How to begin

Consider starting with:

- An important moment that reveals character—yours or someone else's
- A memory or flashback
- A photograph or memento
- Beginnings, endings, first times, last times
- A significant event: illness, birth, death, funeral, wedding, divorce
- A special room and its significance in your life
- Sensory memories: sights, sounds, smells
- Secrets, epiphanies, encounters, accusations
- Arriving somewhere, getting nowhere, on the road
- Successes or failures
- Worst and best moments
- Mentors, heroes, villains

How to make your writing come alive

- Use impressionistic description through metaphorical language: metaphor—direct comparison; simile—metaphor, using *like* or *as* or *as though*.
- Personalize your writing, using "I" words and a subjective approach to subject matter.
- Paint a picture with details and active, descriptive verbs.
- Break your memoir into moments or scenes.

< 78 >

- Capture interesting conversation that reveals something about the character; leave out what's not important.
- Render a scene; boil events down to the basics. What is important to convey? What about you is different because of this incident or time in your life?
- Make your story complex, unpredictable, powerful.
- Use present tense; it gives energy to the writing.
- Orient yourself with the landscape: The external land-scape reflects the inner landscape of your life (turbulent, stormy).
- Do your best to tell the truth as you know it. But even when you're writing about the truth, it's OK to combine several people into a composite character.
- Loop together a series of scenes, such as moments of conflict; this makes writing interesting.

What not to do

- Don't just write down facts; create images.
- Don't tell; show with visual description, dialogue (either conversation you remember verbatim or close to what could have been said based on the situation).
- Don't use clichés and expected language; use powerful verbs.
- Don't weaken your writing with adverbs.
- Don't ramble; compress your language.

A memoir challenges you to do more than recall and record facts about your life. It asks you to reveal yourself, your humanity, and the range of human experience, both joy

< 79 >

and pain. There is something in your story that every reader can relate to, even if you don't know what that will be. Though it is your story, seek universal themes so that it relates not just to you but also to humanity in general.

There are several other kinds of creative nonfiction, including biography, travel and food writing, journaling, literary and political commentary, and essays. Essays are short pieces of prose, usually written from the author's point of view. According to Aldous Huxley, a noted essayist, "Like the novel, the essay is a literary device for saying almost everything about almost anything." A series of essays or commentaries with a unifying theme makes a solid nonfiction book. Former *New York Times* columnist Anna Quindlen has produced three best sellers by bundling her columns.

Remembering What It Takes

1. **Desire:** Now that you've read this far, do you still want to write this book? Are you still wild about the idea and convinced that it will accomplish your purpose, whatever that might be? If so, you have passed one major test. You may have all of the next five things on the list, but without desire, you will not succeed. Keep this particular flame going strong.

2. **A concept:** Does your one-sentence explanation of what your book is about still hold true? You may have changed it along the way, and that's fine as long as you have based your planning on the new version. If the concept changes, review your proposal to be certain it still reflects your

< 80 >

main idea. The proposal will lead seamlessly into the book if that concept is valid. The preface will explain why it matters to you, the introduction will clarify its content and organization, and the chapters will flesh it out and bring it to life.

3. **A plan:** By now, you have completed two aspects of your plan: the proposal and your schedule of deadlines. Thinking that you'll write when you have time will not work. That is why you set deadlines. The third part of planning is to decide when, where, and how much you will write. Don't leave this to chance. Set mini-deadlines within the larger ones. For example, "Every week I will write at least one chapter."

4. **A long attention span:** From beginning to end, planning, writing, publishing, and promoting a book can take anywhere from months to years. I am promising that if you follow the steps in this book, you can do it in six months. If I didn't know it is possible, I wouldn't say it. Publishing and promoting will take more time, but you can apply all the same principles to these aspects of the process. Give yourself a year in all—six months to plan, research, and write and another six months to publish and promote. Then, take stock of where you are. Sticking with such a schedule and maintaining your enthusiasm is what is meant by a long attention span.

5. **Self-discipline:** Staying interested is one thing; actually writing is another. Creating a schedule is a good beginning, but the hard part is sticking with it. (Think exercise program!) Self-discipline is making yourself do

< 81 >

something even on those days that you don't want to. Self-discipline is sticking to your schedule, meeting your deadlines, motivating and re-motivating yourself. Self-discipline is what it takes to write a book in six months … or at all.

6. **Support and guidance:** If you were writing your master's or PhD thesis, you would have an advisor who would push, prod, and hold you accountable for the finished product. If you have an agent or a publisher for your book, you have a similar support system, urging you on and cheerleading when you hit a low point. What if you don't have either? Who will bolster you when you slump, remind you of your mini-deadlines along the way, and pat you on the back when you make them? Earlier, I mentioned writing groups, coaches, classmates, and friends. But there is an even more powerful group to turn to. The concept was originally introduced by Napoleon Hill in his classic *Think and Grow Rich*. He called it a "mastermind group" and described it as a brain trust whose only purposes are to support, encourage, and challenge its members in any and all endeavors. When you form a mastermind group, you seek people who not only will give you advice and feedback but who will also hold you accountable for living up to your commitments. You will do the same for them.

There is one more essential element I want to add:

7. **Small rewards for small victories:** By this time, you have a pretty good idea of what is involved in planning

< 82 >

and writing a book. It takes time, energy, determination, and perseverance. Yes, you can do it in six months, but they are going to be pretty intense months. Ultimately, you create the plan; you set the deadlines; you do the work. And, if you are wise, you reward yourself for every achievement, no matter how small. That can be with a mocha latte or a massage, a day off, or dinner at your favorite restaurant. You have taken on a big job and you deserve it. If you don't reward yourself, who will?

< 83 >

4

STEP 3: PROFESSIONAL PARTNERS

egin by understanding that you will need help bringing your book to fruition. In fact, it's unlikely that you can do it without some of these people.

- Administrative or virtual assistant
- Attorney
- Calligrapher
- Graphic designer
- Distributor
- Editors
- Illustrator
- Indexer
- Industry experts
- Printer
- Publicist
- Reviewers
- Transcriber

< 85 >

- Typographer
- Wholesaler

You will not need everyone on this list, of course, but there are a few in the "must have" column. They include an editor (for concept and content), a copy editor (for grammar, punctuation, and consistency), a graphic designer (for cover and page layout), and a printer. If your book is published by a traditional publisher or a reputable POD house, some of the professionals on the above list will be furnished. If you self-publish, in one form or another, you will have to determine just how much professional assistance you need, where to find the best people for the job, and how much you are willing to pay for their services.

Assembling Your Cast of Characters

• Administrative assistant

An administrative or virtual assistant will become your right hand. At every stage of the process, there will be correspondence, permissions, research, bookkeeping, organization, filing, inventory, publicity, and myriad other necessary details to attend to. You have two choices: Do it all yourself, or hire someone to help you.

• Attorney

An attorney serves several functions, from analyzing contracts to advising you on copyright laws and registering artwork. Talk to a lawyer as you are working on your manuscript. He or she will do the following:

< 86 >

1. Vet (evaluate) your manuscript
2. Negotiate contracts between you and the publisher
3. Keep you out of bad contracts
4. Deal with letters from potential litigants
5. Clarify copyright issues. There is no magic number of words you are allowed to quote or paraphrase. If you have taken the essence of a book, you're in trouble. You definitely need good attribution, and you may well need permission, which you may be charged for.

• Calligrapher

There are two types of calligraphy: alphabetic and pictographic. Alphabetic writing creates words and sentences in specific alphabets such as Arabic, Hebrew, Greek, and Roman. In pictographic writing, symbols or pictograms represent different ideas and words. Chinese and Japanese languages lend themselves to this style. Naturally, this type of writing, like illustration, can be costly and certainly isn't appropriate for every book cover or interior.

• Graphic Designer

I have a colleague who owns a publishing company and insists you have to incorporate quality in your book from the very beginning. He suggests, and I agree, that you give the graphic designer your ideas and let her take it from there. Designers think in pictures; writers think in words. If you and your designer aren't communicating, that's a problem. Your relationship should be synergistic: You know what the message is; she is conveying that message visually. If it isn't

< 87 >

working, end the relationship and keep searching. Often, the same graphic artist can handle both cover design and page layout. Sometimes, however, you will need two separate people. The charges can be relatively small if you use an online design service that specializes in book cover design for self-published authors or a POD house.

They can also become quite costly, depending on the fees of the graphic designer you choose. Conventional publishers will provide cover and page design based on advice from their marketing departments, but often you have little or no input or veto power. Readers spend only seconds looking at a book—first, the cover; then, inside. The interior is very important—so important, in fact, that many experts advise using a graphic designer who specializes in books.

• **Distributor**

Book distributors sell to warehouses and bookstores. They provide a range of services, including electronic ordering systems (EDI), warehousing, fulfillment, shipping, billing, collection, marketing, editorial consultation, and sales. Distributors want 25–30 percent of what they collect from the bookstores, which can take quite a chunk out of the profits. On the other hand, according to Dan Poynter, author of *The Self-Publishing Manual*, "Distribution separates your book from the pack and gives credibility in the marketplace." The following are the best-known distributors: Baker & Taylor for libraries and retail chains; Ingram for retail chains and independent bookstores; Follette for schools; BWI for

< 88 >

children's books; and specialized distributors for special markets.

• Editors

Editors fall into several categories because they work at different stages of the project. A **developmental editor** helps you refine your concept, organize your ideas and your material, and keep yourself on track. A **content editor** looks at the big picture, including writing style, structure, flow of ideas, language, and accuracy. A **copy editor** is the last person to read your manuscript before it is submitted to the publisher and possibly once again in galley form. Copy editors check for grammar, punctuation, and consistency and are invaluable at catching things you and everyone else seem to miss.

For standard rates, check the rate guide of the Editorial Freelancers Association. Two rules to remember: (1) Spell-check is fallible. When in doubt, look it up. And to be sure, buy a speller/divider. (2) Never, ever edit your own work. Find someone interested in your topic. A good editor will question everything.

• Illustrator

Not everyone needs an illustrator. My friend Sharon Winstein, who is working on a trilogy of marvelous cookbooks, hired one illustrator for her covers and another one for inside drawings of food and food preparation. She also engaged a calligrapher to do her title—*Breads, Soups &*

< 89 >

Salads—and inside headings. She is the first to admit it was expensive, but she knew what she wanted, which was superior quality, and she got it.

• Indexer

If your book requires an index, you have two alternatives: your word-processing program or a professional indexer. A conventional publishing house will often provide indexing services. If your book is technical, scientific, fact-filled, or a textbook, you will need an index, and every author and editor I know stresses the importance of hiring a pro to do this job.

• Industry experts

Industry experts, readers, and reviewers may or may not be the same people. Industry experts or readers are professionals who know your subject matter and are willing to give you feedback on how accurately you present this information in your manuscript. Often, they will also provide endorsements that will give your book valuable credibility.

• Printer

Your book must be printed in some form, unless it's an e-book, and you have more to choose from than ever before. If your book is being published by a conventional or independent publisher, this won't be your responsibility. If you are self-publishing, obviously it will. The kind of printing you select will range in both sophistication and price. At one end is taking the file to a quick-copy store and telling them how

< 90 >

many copies you want. Then, you can have it bound on the spot in a number of ways.

At the other end is a high-quality, four-color, offset printer that can reproduce beautiful photographs. Chances are you will be somewhere in the middle. If you plan to have more than 500 copies printed and stored in your home or in a warehouse, you would choose a high-quality offset printer. If you would rather have a small number of copies printed as you need them, digital printing is a good choice. Bear in mind that POD "publishers" are sometimes only glorified digital printers.

• Publicist

Not every author has a publicist. Quite often, you will wear that hat in addition to all the others. The important point is that you must market your book, usually well before it finds its way into print. A publicist saves you a lot of legwork by arranging for travel, radio and TV appearances, book signings, interviews, and articles in various publications.

• Reviewers

Reviewers are usually affiliated with some form of media. They assess the quality of the writing, how well and logically you cover the topic, and how readable the book is. A positive review is like gold that can be mined in many ways, one of which is to quote the reviewer on the back cover.

• Transcriber

If you record your interviews, you will find it terribly

< 91 >

time-consuming to transcribe every one yourself. Another option is voice-recognition software. The best for PCs is Dragon Naturally Speaking; for Macs, the latest is Mac-Speech Dictate. As you speak, the software generates hard copy. One caveat: You have to train voice recognition software (no surprise) to recognize your voice.

• Typographer

Typographers are an endangered species because most of us create our books on computers and submit the file to a designer, a POD house, or a publisher. Poof! Digital magic. But when you want something very special, you need an artisan with type; you can still find one if you look.

• Wholesaler

Wholesalers handle books based on demand. They carry books from most publishers and fill orders as they receive them. Their main service is delivering books quickly; they do not have sales reps. There are several categories of wholesalers, including national, regional, specialized, and library.

< 92 >

ESTIMATED COSTS: SELF-PUBLISHING A NONFICTION BOOK

Professional Partners	Planning		Writing		Production		Publishing		Promotion	
	Estimated Costs	Actual Costs	Estimated Costs	Actual Costs	Estimated Costs	Actual Costs	Estimated Costs	Actual Costs	Estimated Costs	Actual Costs
Admin / virtual assistant	$25 to $60 / hr									
Attorney			$150 to $350 / hr							
Book coach	$75 to $300 / hr									
Copy editor (1 page = 300 words)			$4 to $10 / page or $18 to $35 / hr							
Developmental editor			$10 to $12 / page or $75 to $125 / hr							
Ghostwriter			$20,000 to $50,000							
Designer (cover)					$450 to $650					
Designer (interior)					$5 to $15 per page					
Distributor							Nominal registration fee + 55% of profit			
Illustrator							Discretion of artist			
Indexer							$2 to $5* per indexable page **			
Industry experts			Discretion of expert							
Photographer							$500 to $10,000			

< 93 >

ESTIMATED COSTS: SELF-PUBLISHING A NONFICTION BOOK

Professional Partners	Planning		Writing		Production		Publishing		Promotion	
	Estimated Costs	Actual Costs	Estimated Costs	Actual Costs	Estimated Costs	Actual Costs	Estimated Costs	Actual Costs	Estimated Costs	Actual Costs
Proofreader (1 page = 300 words)							$2 to $3.75 typeset page or $15 to $25 /hr			
Printer / binder							500 books: $3.55 to $5.25 per book 1,000 books: $2.36 to $3.50 per book			
Proposal development	$3,000 to $5,000									
Publicist / marketing consultant									$75 to $300 per hour	
Reviewers									Free copy of book, no charge for review	
Website designer									$1,500 to $5,000	
Total										

*Rate is variable depending upon subject matter and type of book (e.g., Dense scholarly, heavily footnoted works will cost more than a children's book). Depending on the indexer, rate is quite negotiable.

** Indexable page does not include front matter or bibliography. Includes endnotes only if they contain additional substantive material that adds to the content of the text.

< 94 >

Professional Partners Worksheet

Administrative assistant
Name:
Phone:
Fax:
E-mail:

Attorney
Name:
Phone:
Fax:
E-mail:

Calligrapher
Name:
Phone:
Fax:
E-mail:

Content editor
Name:
Phone:
Fax:
E-mail:

< 95 >

Copy editor
Name:
Phone:
Fax:
E-mail:

Cover designer
Name:
Phone:
Fax:
E-mail:

Distribution center
Name:
Phone:
Fax:
E-mail:

Illustrator
Name:
Phone:
Fax:
E-mail:

Indexer
Name:
Phone:
Fax:
E-mail:

< 96 >

Industry experts

Name:

Phone:

Fax:

E-mail:

Page-layout designer

Name:

Phone:

Fax:

E-mail:

Printer

Name:

Phone:

Fax:

E-mail:

Publicist

Name:

Phone:

Fax:

E-mail:

Reviewers

Name:

Phone:

Fax:

E-mail:

< 97 >

Transcriber
Name:
Phone:
Fax:
E-mail:

Typographer
Name:
Phone:
Fax:
E-mail:

Wholesaler
Name:
Phone:
Fax:
E-mail:

< 98 >

5

STEP 4: PRODUCTION

Production is the unglamorous aspect of publishing. Books do not go directly from manuscript to printed page; there are a number of steps in between. Covers and page layouts must be designed, proofs read and reread, production details ironed out, and changes made when necessary (it will almost always be necessary). If your book is published traditionally, much of that will be handled for you; but even then, you will spend hours reviewing, correcting, and re-reviewing every element. If you self-publish, of course, these details are totally your responsibility and require a great deal of time and careful attention. Here is a quick review of the production details you spelled out in your proposal.

- Book length: rounded off in double-spaced pages or word count

< 99 >

- Delivery date: expressed in three-month increments or upon receipt of advance
- Computer: type of computer and word-processing program
- Form in which you will submit manuscript (PDF, word-processing file, upload, or CD-ROM)
- Format: any special preferences in size, binding, treatment of text
- Sidebars: estimated number and content
- Permissions: how many, who, actual or estimated fees
- Front matter: copyright page, dedication, foreword, preface, acknowledgments, and introduction (Include only what you plan to have.)
- Back matter: appendices, glossary, references, bibliography, index, (Include only what you plan to have.)
- Endorsements: who has committed to write one, potential endorsements, or people to contact
- Resources needed to complete your book: itemized expenses, travel, long-distance calls, permissions, editing, etc.
- Photographs and artwork (number of files, form of submission, e.g., high-resolution scans)

< 100 >

Production Details Worksheet

Book length: rounded off in double-spaced pages or word count

Delivery date: expressed in three-month increments or upon receipt of advance

Type of computer and word-processing program

Form in which you will submit manuscript (PDF, word-processing file, upload, or CD ROM)

Format: any special preferences in size, binding, treatment of text

< 101 >

Sidebars: estimated number and content

Permissions: how many, who, actual or estimated fees
1.
2.
3.

Front matter: foreword, preface, introduction, dedication, acknowledgments (only what you plan to have in the book)

Back matter: index, bibliography, resource directory, glossary, appendices (only what you will have)

< 102 >

Endorsements (on hand, anticipated)
1.
2.
3.

Resources needed to complete your book
1.
2.
3.

Photographs and artwork (number of pieces; how they will
be submitted)

< 103 >

STEP 5: PUBLISHING

Publishing is exciting because it means your book is finally going to become "real" and tangible. Yet, this is the part that so often derails even the most passionate and determined author. One reason is that many authors struggle through the writing and then suddenly have a finished manuscript and nowhere to send it. If you are one of them, it may be that you started in the middle (Writing) instead of at the beginning (Planning). It is rarely necessary to write the whole book before approaching a conventional publisher. A proposal and a couple of sample chapters are usually sufficient. There are six publishing options.

1. Conventional or traditional
You have three choices here: (1) You submit a proposal to a recognized publishing company, and it is accepted; (2) you

< 105 >

submit a query letter or proposal to a literary agent, and he or she expresses interest; or (3) the publisher assigns the book to you as a writer for hire and pays you a set fee. In all cases, the publisher assumes all publishing responsibilities and expenses. The publishing industry is highly competitive, and many of the larger houses are gobbling up the smaller ones. Publishers are in business to make money, and they look at your book as a commodity. They ask one question: Will it sell?

2. Self-publishing

You take on these responsibilities by forming your own publishing company. For advice on how to do this, check out the Independent Book Publishers Association (IBPA) or its local chapter in your city. Be sure to read Dan Poynter's book *The Self-Publishing Manual: How to Write, Print and Sell Your Book* and *The Well-Fed Publisher* by Peter Bowerman. As a self-publisher, you are responsible for printing, warehousing, marketing, and distributing your books.

3. Print-on-demand (POD) / Author services companies

While several companies call themselves POD "publishers," *POD is actually a digital technology.* It is an excellent option if you want to print anywhere from 1 to 500 books at a time. The rest of the time, your book is stored as a digital file on a large server. This eliminates the need for sizeable press runs and storage space. Most POD/author services companies, such as Dog Ear, LuLu, and CreateSpace, offer a variety

< 106 >

of packages to authors and contract out the actual printing to LightningSource or some other digital printer.

4. Independent publishers

These are generally small houses that handle from ten to twenty titles a year, usually in a few selected genres, such as African-American literature, spirituality, inspiration, religion, etc. An "indie" publisher must put out at least ten ISBNs a year to be accepted by a major distributor such as Ingram or Baker & Taylor. This a growing segment of the publishing world.

5. Electronic or digital publishing

Your book is published as an electronic or e-book through an e-publisher, on your own website, or on CDs. Or it can be self-published and distributed through other appropriate websites. E-publishing looked as if it might be the wave of the future, but it languished a while and seemed to be going nowhere. Now, due to new technology and renewed interest, it is having a resurgence. Amazon's Kindle and Fire, Barnes & Noble's Nook, Apple's iPad, and Sony represent the newest technology in e-publishing, and they are racing to become the undisputed leader of the pack.

6. Do nothing

Ninety-five percent of authors do nothing. That means more than 400,000 manuscripts go unpublished each year because when authors get to this point, they simply stop.

< 107 >

Publishing Options

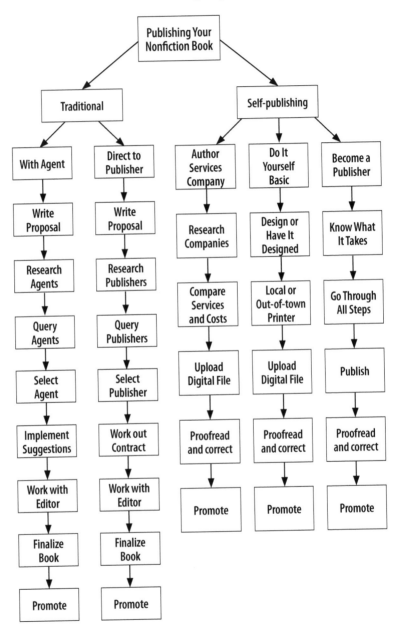

< 108 >

Conventional or Traditional

How do you choose? Well, you start by knowing the advantages and disadvantages of each one and evaluating which seems to be the best fit. For example, having a major publisher's name on the spine of your book is impressive, but it comes with a price. Writing a formal proposal can seem intimidating because it poses so many questions that must be answered at the outset and, of course, the writing must be excellent.

You relinquish control of many aspects of your book to the publisher, which makes decisions based on input from its marketing department. An editor will be assigned to you, and that person may ask you to make some changes. The process takes much longer than self-publishing and, contrary to what you may think, much of the promotion will still be up to you.

Advantages of submitting to a conventional publisher

- Credibility as an author because the book was put out by a major publisher
- Publisher-assigned professional editor, indexer, and proofreader
- Some publisher-arranged publicity and promotion
- Access to major book warehouses, such as Ingram and Baker & Taylor
- Financial advance on royalties (usually small), which is recouped when (and if) the book sells

< 109 >

Why use an agent?

Many publishers will no longer accept a proposal unless it comes from an agent. While agents don't guarantee that your book will be published, they can ensure that it gets a reading. They also advocate for you throughout the process. You can find the right agent for you, if you know where to look.

How to find an agent

• Start online by looking up The Association of Authors' Representatives (AAR), a not-for-profit organization of qualified literary agents. AAR serves as a resource for its members and protects their best interests. AAR agents are obligated to uphold integrity and the highest professional standards in all of their business dealings. Do not consider an agent who does not meet the rigorous standards of the AAR and the National Writers Union (NWU).

• Check out online and print directories. Jeff Herman's book *Writer's Guide to Book Editors, Publishers, and Literary Agents* is invaluable. His online directory also lists agents' e-mail addresses and websites. *Writer's Digest Books' Guide to Literary Agents, Literary Market Place (LMP)*, and *The Directory of the American Book Publishing Industry* are also excellent sources and may be all you need.

• Hardcover and trade paperback publishers produce catalogs, which often include agents' names and contact information. These are sent to booksellers, libraries, and sales

< 110 >

reps. Browse bookstore shelves in the sections where your book might be. Check the dedication and acknowledgments section of competitive books to see whether the authors have thanked their editors and agents.

- If the media are hyping your book, agents will find you. Your job is to be sure the media know about it.

- And network, network, network. Go where writers and agents are likely to be, such as writing classes, readings, lectures, seminars, book signings, conferences, and book festivals. Join writers' organizations and attend meetings. Talk to people who have been published. Ask whether they have used an agent, and don't hesitate to request referrals. In my experience, writers are generous folks who are more than willing to share such information and support each other.

In this age of specialization, literary agents are no exception. Like doctors, they have specific niches. When you do research—whether it is in the reference room of your public library or online—begin with your particular genre. There's no sense sending a query letter or proposal to someone who is not an expert in that area of nonfiction. Narrowing your search will increase your odds of success.

An agent will do the following:
- Critique your book proposal before it is submitted and make suggestions or edits to help you improve it.

< 111 >

- Know which publishers are likely to be interested in your proposal.
- Garner attention for your proposal and sell it faster than you can.
- Act as your business representative and, as such, protect your best interests, secure advances, settle contract disputes, collect money, review royalty statements, and ensure that publishers meet their contractual obligations.
- Become your support system, guide, and cheerleader, which every author needs.
- Bring a new editor up to date on you and your book if that becomes necessary.
- Earn money only when he or she sells your book proposal, which is a great motivator.
- Become your closest ally in the publishing process.

What do agents want from you?

When I first decided to submit a book to an agent, I looked online and found two of the biggest and best-known agents: Michael Larsen and Elizabeth Pomada. Michael Larsen is the author of *How to Get a Literary Agent, How to Write a Book Proposal,* and *Guerilla Marketing for Writers: 100 Weapons to Help You Sell Your Book.* I wrote to Larsen and Pomada, and they replied with a sheaf of requirements to fulfill before they would even look at my book. It was intimidating but instructive. One thing stood out in my mind: You have to prove to an agent that there is a market for your

< 112 >

book, that you know how to reach that market, and that you will work tirelessly to do so.

One thing most agents want is a solid query letter, which takes a great deal of thought and often many revisions. A query letter is not something you dash off. The agent wants to know not only what your book is about and why you are qualified to write it but also how well you write. This letter may be the most important piece of marketing you will do. It has four parts:

1. The grabber

This is your opening paragraph, and it has to grab your reader and hold on. If you have been referred by a client, mention that. If your book fits in the agent's or publisher's particular niche, by all means say so. At the very least, this paragraph should contain your "book hook"—one or two sentences that not only explain what your book is about but also sum up the essence of the story. The grabber pulls the reader in and elicits a response, which should be interest and curiosity. If you have written a powerful concept statement, you already have your book hook.

Here are a few examples of book hooks:

The freedom and independence of a freelance writer's life are only half the story; the other half includes the practical realities of finding work, writing well on demand, and managing a business—all at the same time.

< 113 >

Dealing with difficult people in the workplace is a given; it takes people skills and practice to build and sustain productive relationships with peers, supervisors, and others on or off the job.

Ask any ten successful women these questions—What does success mean to you? How have you achieved it? What advice would you give other women?—and you will get ten completely different answers.

In her early teens, Jane Doe suffered a devastating depression that came on with no warning and signaled the beginning of a lifelong battle with bipolar disorder, a condition that was not diagnosed until she reached adulthood.

2. Explaining your message

This is your opportunity to answer the questions an agent or publisher might have after being captivated by your book hook. It is a synopsis with punch, your book boiled down to a short paragraph. What is the book's purpose? What are its main points? Why is it important and timely? If your hook is your elevator speech, consider this paragraph what you might say if you and the other person traveled a few more floors together.

3. About the author

What would an agent or publisher want to know about you as it pertains to your book? Are you an expert on this

< 114 >

subject, and, if so, what makes you one? Here is your chance to explain your qualifications and writing credentials. If your education is relevant to the subject, include it; otherwise, leave it out. Have you been published? Where? Have you won any awards? Has your work been reviewed? Keep this paragraph focused on your experience.

4. Action step

Your closing paragraph should be short and simple. Express your appreciation for the reader's time and consideration of your submission. Include a complete book proposal or an outline and sample chapter and your contact information. Mention a date when you will follow up with a phone call.

How to deal with an agent once you have one

According to Lori Perkins, author of *The Insider's Guide to Getting an Agent* (Writers' Digest Books), there are ways to treat an agent and ways not to. On the plus side of the ledger are simple courtesies like saying thank you; keeping the agent posted on developments as they occur; educating yourself about the publishing industry; and, though it should seem obvious, always being completely honest.

On the other hand...

- Don't expect miracles or the impossible. It's in everyone's best interest to sell your book.
- Don't second-guess their decisions. Agents will do everything possible to make you feel special and to get you a good deal.

< 115 >

- When the deal doesn't meet your expectations, don't shoot the messenger.
- Don't be pushy about money or contracts. Pressure doesn't speed up the process.
- Don't expect your agent to teach you to write, advance you money, or act as your attorney, therapist, or publicist.
- Finally, if your agent thinks you need to do more work on your book or proposal, don't be a prima donna. Ridley Pearson, the best-selling mystery writer, tells a story about a writer he referred to his agent. When the agent suggested some changes, the writer took offense and refused. He never got his book published, by the way.

Self-publishing

This is the subject of so many books, it is hardly possible to do more than hit the high points here. *The most important thing to know is that you do everything a publisher does, and you pay for all of it.* On the other hand, if there is a profit after expenses, you keep it. A second point is that you can make a lot of mistakes and spend a lot of unnecessary money if you don't know what you're doing. So, how do you become an instant expert? Frankly, there is no such thing as "instant." Publishing a book is a complex process, and when you've never done it before, it can seem like feeling your way around a maze wearing a blindfold.

Who self-publishes?
1. People with a story to tell
2. People seeking fame
3. Academics and educators

< 116 >

4. Entertainers
5. Entrepreneurs who want to promote their businesses
6. People who wish to be considered subject-matter experts
7. Trainers and seminar facilitators
8. Professional speakers
9. Authors who are seeking an agent or publisher

Why self-publish?

- Your proposal was rejected by conventional publishers.
- You want complete control of design, speed of publication, profits, and promotion.
- You can command higher speaker fees.
- You will earn additional income from back-of-the-room sales.
- The process is faster than conventional publishing.
- You will learn the publishing business.

Why not self-publish?

- There will be out-of-pocket expenditures for all aspects of publishing: graphic design, ISBN, printing, promotion, and more.
- You will need to learn the publishing business, often from the ground up.
- You will spend a great deal of time and energy on marketing.

What it really means to be a "publisher"

The idea of self-publishing is very appealing to many new

< 117 >

authors, who often have no idea what is expected from them. To clear up any misunderstanding on this issue, the board of directors of International Book Publishers Association (IBPA) drafted a ten-step checklist for publishers, posted it on its website, and summarized it in an article in the IBPA newsletter. Written by former executive director Jan Nathan, "What Is a Publisher? And Why You Might Not Count as One" spelled out the criteria for being a bona fide publisher.

"The most basic requirement for becoming a publisher," wrote Nathan, "is purchasing a series of ISBNs from R.R. Bowker Company and making sure that your company is the publisher of record for them."

But that is only one requirement. Even if you are the author, you are expected to develop a business plan with a budget, accept financial responsibility for producing and promoting the book, create a contract that spells out what the author does and what the publisher does, fulfill all the technical aspects of publishing, have the book professionally designed and edited, and deal with all relevant industry-related vendors.

Self-publishing 101

What follows are the absolute basics of what you need to know, do, or have as a self-publisher:

- Start with a great title and subtitle. You're going to need it every step of the way. This is harder than it sounds, and it's important enough to hire an expert to guide you. One of the best is Sam Horn (http://www.samhorn.com/).

< 118 >

- Have your book cover designed by a graphic designer who specializes in books. Peggy Nehmen is my designer of choice. She designed this book, as well as my last book, *Words To Live By: Reflections on the writing life from a 40-year veteran.* (http://www.n-kcreative.com).

- Go to your favorite bookstore and look at book covers. What grabs your attention? What turns you off? What is boring? What feels good in your hand? Share your impressions with your book designer.

- Write a marketing plan. It is never too early, and you can always add to it as you go along. In its simplest form, a marketing plan starts with an overall goal for what you want to accomplish, strategies for how you plan to do it, and specific tactics or actions you will take, with target dates and estimated costs. There are many book-marketing sites. Here are three good ones:
  http://www.websitemarketingplan.com/
  http://book-promotion.blogspot.com/
  http://www.bob-baker.com/self-publish-book/blog

- Create a promotional piece or brochure. Here is one time you will be grateful for the time you put into drafting your proposal because you will have all the information you need at your fingertips.

< 119 >

- Put together a mailing list. You should already have one, but this is the time to prune and add to it. A solid mailing list is a must-have for authors. You need one for snail mail and another for e-mail.

- Develop a website for your book. It doesn't have to be elaborate, but it should entice and inform. Add to it as you are further along in the process. Hire an expert, or try your hand at doing it yourself. These programs all received top reviews from http://www.consumersearch.com/: Dream-Weaver 8, CoffeeCup 2006 for Windows, Homestead Site-Builder, and WordPress 2.0.

- Create a blog to keep people informed of your progress and establish yourself as an expert on your topic. There are a host of blog sites to choose from that make it fairly easy to set up your own blog and customize your message. Just Google or Yahoo "create blog," or check out Blogger and WordPress.

- Choose a name for your publishing company (you may have to file a fictitious name statement). Expert Dan Poynter suggests that having a book written, published, and distributed by the author detracts from the book's credibility.

- Download or send for copyright form CO-instructions and file the forms with the U.S. Copyright Office (http://www.copyright.gov/forms). Even though your work is

< 120 >

automatically copyrighted when you write it, this is an added protection.

- Print it out, and sign it.
  Send all required copies with a check for $50 to
  Library of Congress
  Copyright Office
  101 Independence Avenue SE
  Washington, DC 20559

- Check into the need for local business licenses; apply for them if necessary.

- Secure an ISBN (International Standard Book Number) from R.R. Bowker (www.bowker.com). You can buy only one ISBN or blocks of 10, 100, or more. If you plan to write more than one book or develop spin-off products for your present book, buy at least ten. Some printers provide ISBNs, but be sure they are in *your name, not the printer's.* You will also need an International Article Number (EAN) bar code, which you can also get from Bowker.

- Have your manuscript edited and copy edited (remember, they are not the same thing) before it goes into design. Have page proofs proofread by a *fresh* set of eyes. I cannot stress this enough.

- Send out advance review copies (ARCs) of galleys to appropriate publications and reviewers (see page 91).

< 121 >

Crane's Duplicating specializes in ARCs (http://www. boundgalleys.com). Mark them as readers copies. (Don't send a published book.)

- Request testimonials to include in the book, on the cover, and in your promotional materials.

- Research all of your options on digital printers, POD companies, and offset printers. Lightning Source is a printer that deals only with publishers. It is owned by Ingram, one of the largest distributors in the U.S. and the UK.

- Get competitive quotes from printers (be sure they are all bidding on the same specs), and choose the one that best meets your needs, including but not limited to price.

- Decide how you want to handle storage and distribution. You can do both if you have room and time, but choosing a professional distributor and fulfillment house will save you time and many trips to the post office.

- When you receive your printed books, examine them very carefully for appearance, consistency, quality, pages, and printing—in short, everything. Don't settle for less than perfect. Once you sign the printer's release form and the books are printed, *you own them.* If there are mistakes, *you* are responsible.

- Do a promotional mailing. This is when all your hard work on your brochure and mailing list pays off.

< 122 >

- Set up a "press or media room" on your website so that media can find the information they need in a form they can use.

- Write articles on your subject; submit articles to print publications and online article sites. There are countless such sites, but the undisputed leader of the pack is www. ezinearticles.com.

- Think of book promotion as an ongoing, full-time job. The more promotion you do, the more successful your book will be.

- Consider fresh ways to repackage your content; develop spin-off products (CDs, DVDs, reports, mini-books, podcasts, e-books, website content).

There is little doubt that being your own publisher is a big job but also one that brings creative autonomy, satisfaction, and profits. Before you tackle it, be very sure you have the time, energy, and money.

Print-on-Demand (POD)/Author Services

POD is an increasingly popular technology that makes it possible to print anywhere from 1 to 500 books at a time. The appeal of most author services companies, such as CreateSpace (owned by Amazon) and BookLocker, Cold Tree Press, Lulu, and Infinity Press is that they offer a variety of packages to authors.

< 123 >

The setup fees and cost per book or per page vary from publisher to publisher, so it's a good idea to shop around. Obviously, the quality of the books produced this way runs the gamut. It is up to the author to ensure that the book meets the same high standards demanded by conventional publishers. Since that doesn't always happen, the value of being a "published author" may be compromised. It won't take many obviously inferior books to give POD the same poor reputation once attached to "vanity press."

There is a lot of confusion about POD, which author Mark Levine clears up in his well-researched book, *The Fine Print of Self-Publishing: The Contracts & Services of 45 Self-Publishing Companies Analyzed, Ranked & Exposed* (Fourth Edition). This book answers the questions most authors don't know enough to ask. Dan Poynter's front-cover testimonial says, "It will save you a lot of time, money, and heartache." That's quite an endorsement.

Benefits of POD
1. You can tell your story the way you want to.
2. You retain the rights to your book.
3. You retain editorial/creative control.
4. You still receive a royalty.
5. Your book can be a means to an end or an end in itself.
6. You can say you are an author.

Disadvantages of POD
- POD is a technology—shorthand for digital printing; it is not a publisher.

< 124 >

- Most POD companies charge an upfront fee, which can be as high as $1,500.
- Most POD companies have strict guidelines for format, size, and pricing.
- There are additional charges for editing and marketing; sometimes, the marketing package is mandatory.
- If the company designs the covers, it owns the design.
- Wholesalers and retailers may not buy POD books because they are nonreturnable, higher in price, and often lower in quality.
- While POD is far better than vanity press, the principle is similar: books are printed as submitted for a fee and are not subject to editorial quality control.
- The author has little control over production; quality of printing varies from one company to another.
- The ISBN is often in the company's name, not the author's, making the company the publisher of record.
- After an initial number of complimentary books, authors must purchase copies of their own books at about 40 percent of retail.

Independent Publishing

As the number of conventional publishers shrinks, the ranks of independent publishers swell. Independent publishers are generally small and cater to particular niche markets. Since it is becoming more difficult to gain acceptance from a major publisher, "indie" publishers are becoming a very viable option. Four thousand publishers belong to the Independent Book Publishers Association (IBPA), the trade

< 125 >

association that serves book, audio, and video publishers in the United States and around the world. The IBPA'S mission is to advance the professional interests of its members—regardless of their size or experience—through cooperative marketing programs, education, information, and advocacy within the industry.

Electronic or Digital Publishing
What is digital publishing?

Electronic publishing, or e-publishing, includes the digital publication of e-books and electronic articles as well as the development of digital libraries and catalogues. In addition to distribution on the Internet (also known as online or Web publishing), there are many electronic, technical, and reference publications on CD and DVD for users who do not have reliable and high-speed access to a network.

Where can you find e-book/online publishers?

There is a difference between e-book publishers and online publishers. When you do a Google search for e-book publishers, you get a smorgasbord of POD or author services companies, all of which digitally print or farm out the digital printing of your PDF files. If you want your book online, supposedly they will publish it there; if you want it on paper, they will print it and sell it to you at a discounted price.

On the other hand, if you do a search for online publishers, you end up at Online Publishers Association (OPA), which represents the highest standards in online publishing and has sixty current members, including NPR, PBS, *The*

< 126 >

Wall Street Journal, The New York Times, Time, The Huffington Post, and Reuters. This does not seem to be helpful to authors.

What are e-book readers?

Amazon was the first to enter the digital market with Kindle, its wireless e-book reader. Kindle makes available more than 350,000 books, newspapers, magazines, and blogs. Amazon's newest product, Fire, is an e-reader and virtual entertainment center all in one. It is expected to offer Apple's iPad some stiff competition. Other popular e-book readers are Sony, Barnes & Noble's Nook, and Kobo Wireless e-reader. These devices continue to evolve and improve, as they get thinner, larger, and easier to read. Most are in color now and store music and photos, show movies, and offer a wide range of games. With some of these devices you can download directly from the Web and take e-books out of the library.

There had been other forays into the world of digital books years ago. They failed due to incompatible e-book readers and digital platforms and competition that did itself in. This time it looks as if the whole e-book industry is here to stay.

The good news for readers is that prices keep going down. Kindle, which started out at $269, is now $79. By the time this book is published, it may be even lower. It's good news for authors, too, since we can digitize our books and sell them in the Kindle store. Kindle has a proprietary platform and does not accept ePub, which most of the others

< 127 >

use. Smashwords (http://www.smashwords.com) and Book-baby (http://www.bookbaby.com) will convert your book to all formats, which will save you a great deal of stress if you are not a techie.

If you are converting your own book, you will have to let go of your need to control fonts, sizes, page numbers, images, etc., mainly because readers can adjust the fonts on their electronic readers (such as the Kindle). So the text flows based on the user's preferences, not yours. Images are tricky. You can insert them, but often they are small and difficult to read. Technology is advancing, and this too will probably be temporary.

Do Nothing

I hope this one doesn't need a lot of explanation. Of course, there are many reasons why an author would abandon ship at the publishing stage of the process. If you have come this far, though, I hope you won't find any of them to be persuasive.

Reason 1: You don't want to give up control of your brain-child. You have choices, even with a traditional publisher. Unless you abdicate all control by signing your life away without reading the contract, remember, you are the author. So, if you are given a contract, hire an attorney. It is worth the cost! In fact, if you receive a contract for any reason, hire an attorney.

< 128 >

Reason 2: You have no money to purchase any of the options that have a fee. Well, you could wait until you do have it. Putting it off is not the same as doing nothing. You could borrow it, but if you decide to go into debt, remember that printing is only one of the major expenses you will incur. One last word: Do not use a credit card to finance your book!

Reason 3: You've run out of steam or enthusiasm. You can't go through the publishing process when you are burned out. So, take a break to regroup, refresh, and rethink—anywhere from a couple of hours to a couple of weeks.

< 129 >

7

STEP 6: PROMOTION

Promoting or marketing your book is a good news–bad news story. The bad news is that it is not for the faint-hearted. It takes work, perseverance, imagination, and often money. The good news is that there are *1001 Ways to Market Your Books*, which is the title of the best-selling book by John Kremer. (If I knew that you were going to rush right out and buy it, I wouldn't even write this section.)

First, you should know that publishers routinely handle placement with distributors and bookstores, as well as limited promotion. If you are a best-selling author, they may arrange book tours, signings, and appearances on talk shows. If you are not a best-selling author (yet), expect to do much or all of the marketing yourself.

Let's say you are starting from scratch and have no idea where to begin. Gather five or six people who think outside

< 131 >

the box and will be honest with you. Make it a party; serve refreshments. Then, tape two big sheets of paper to the wall. One is a chart with boxes (see page 135); the other is a big sheet of blank paper (you can use a flip chart instead). The goal of this exercise is to create your book marketing plan by filling in the boxes on the chart.

How to Write a Book Marketing Plan

Writing a book marketing plan is not rocket science. In fact, it is a game of filling in the boxes. There are 15 boxes on the chart. Each one has a purpose.

The foundation of your plan

There are three boxes across the top of your map. The first says, "**My book is about...**" The second is **your book's purpose** or what you want your book to achieve. The third describes **your ideal reader.** Way back in the beginning of this book, when I walked you through the steps necessary to write your proposal, you answered all of these questions. Now fill in the top three boxes on the wall chart. You are the only one at the party who can do this part of the exercise.

These three boxes should become your measuring stick for everything you do from this point forward. When you are considering a marketing activity, ask yourself these two questions: Will this help me achieve my book's purpose? Will this be an effective way to connect with my ideal reader? If the answers are no or I'm not sure, table the idea for now.

< 132 >

Strategies

The next three boxes are called strategies. They are big-picture objectives or policies designed to achieve your purpose. The brainstorming begins here. First, explain to the group what "strategies" are. Once everyone understands what the boxes are for, they will shout out ideas. You want to generate as many ideas as possible. Nobody criticizes anybody else's thinking. No idea is too off the wall. Let the suggestions fly, and just write them on the big sheet of paper or flip chart as fast as you hear them. When you are completely out of ideas, evaluate the results. Which ones will help you achieve your purpose and reach your ideal reader? Choose three strategies, and fill in the second set of boxes.

Sample strategies

1. Use your book to increase visibility and credibility.
2. Use your book to increase demand for your professional services or other products.
3. Use your business to increase demand for the book.
4. Sell online through website and other online booksellers.
5. Sell to businesses to give to employees.
6. Reach your ideal readers through various book formats.
7. Put your book on social networking sites.
8. Spread the word through public relations campaign(s).
9. Increase exposure with online marketing campaign(s).
10. Create direct-to-reader marketing campaigns.

< 133 >

Tactics

Back to brainstorming. Under each strategy box are three little boxes, labeled Tactic. These are your action steps—what you will do to achieve each strategy. Repeat the same practice to come up with actionable items. Make them specific and attainable. Choose the best ones, and fill in the rest of your chart.

Sample tactics

Specific activities to put your strategies into action:

1. Reuse content: Publish articles in trade publications; write and submit articles through your website and on online article sites.
2. Offer books for sale at your seminars, workshops, public speaking engagements, and other points of contact with potential customers.
3. Offer branded bookmarks, how-to articles, and tips.
4. Sell customized editions to companies (with minimum order) as gifts to employees and company's customers.
5. Create press release; participate in media interviews.

What follows is the book marketing chart. You can enlarge it or simply draw your own version on a sheet of paper. Go over your brainstorming list and choose the best ideas. Remember the difference between strategies (objectives) and tactics (actions). Fill in your chart and start promoting your book.

< 134 >

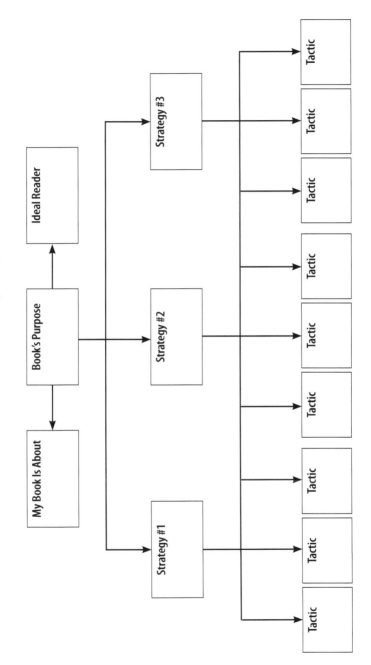

Book Marketing Map

My Book Is About — Book's Purpose — Ideal Reader

Strategy #1 — Strategy #2 — Strategy #3

Tactic — Tactic — Tactic — Tactic — Tactic — Tactic — Tactic — Tactic — Tactic

< 135 >

Nine ways to build an author platform

A new buzzword in the publishing business is "author platform." Your platform is your sphere of "influence," your ability to sell books to your market. When you write your book proposal, you must tell the reader (agent, acquisition editor, or publisher) who your connections are and how you are going to reach your target market.

A platform is organic: it grows over time. And it is valuable. I recently heard a speaker explaining the word "platform" to an eager audience. He had his typed on a single sheet of paper. He told us we could look at it, but we could not have a copy. Then, of course, we all wanted to see it. It was a list—a very detailed list. If you can answer the following questions, you can build your own list.

- Are you a celebrity or a household name? Have you been in the news? Are you the CEO of a well-known corporation? Have you achieved celebrity status for the "wrong" reasons?
- Are you a professional speaker? Are you paid a substantial fee to speak? Do you attract large audiences? Do they pay to hear your presentations?
- Do you have a popular blog or website that reaches thousands of people? Do they follow or subscribe to your blog?
- Do they leave comments, and do you respond, thus creating a dialogue?
- Do you have a way to capture e-mail addresses and build a large list of subscribers—an e-zine, a newsletter, or regular promotions with free give-aways?

< 136 >

- Do you podcast to a large and enthusiastic audience? Can you promote your book to them?
- Are you on social networking sites—Facebook, MySpace, LinkedIn, Twitter, YouTube? Do you have lots of friends, network connections, followers, and subscribers? Will they buy your book?
- Are you already a published author with an established readership? Did you self-publish your book or books and market them effectively online or in the bricks-and-mortar world?
- Do you belong to organizations or associations related to your topic? Do you know other members? Can you access the membership list?
- Do you have raving fans, former students, clients, friends, or family members who will not only buy your book but also tell everyone they know how great it is?

If you answered yes to any of those questions, you have the beginning of a powerful platform. Keep building it!

Common promotional practices

You don't have to reinvent the wheel to promote your book. There are already many accepted ways to do it. Some cost money; others just require lots of energy and shoe leather.

Advance review copies (ARCs)

ARCs are uncorrected galley proofs that are stamped "readers copy" and then sent to reviewers. The most important review editors are with trade review magazines within the

< 137 >

book industry. They are listed in *Literary Market Place* in the reference room at most libraries. ARCs should also be sent to magazine and newspaper book reviewers, book review syndicates, columnists, radio and television stations, and book clubs. Your reference librarian can lead you to information on all of these and more.

Advertising

Advertising costs money and isn't always as effective as you might suppose. If you are going to advertise, research the media to be sure they are targeting the same audience you are. If your audience is writers, for example, your choices range from inexpensive newsletters to such national writers magazines as *Writer's Digest* and *The Writer.* Be selective.

Amazon

If you have a book, whether it is traditionally or self-published, potential readers expect it to be on Amazon. This is just a fact of life for authors. You may be in Barnes & Noble; you may have a shopping cart on your website; you may be selling your book out of the trunk of your car. You still need a presence on Amazon.

According to Wikipedia, amazon.com is America's largest online retailer, with nearly three times the Internet sales revenue of the runner-up, Staples. In other words, it is a force—a force that can help you sell books.

Amazon is much more than a huge, virtual bookstore. Besides the many other tangible products it sells, its greatest value may be in the ways it can sell YOU. In fact, you can

< 138 >

promote yourself on Amazon even if you don't have a book listed on the site. Here are just a few ways to do so.

- Well-thought-out customer reviews
- A powerful reviewer profile
- Amazon discussion forums
- Your own blog
- Friends on Amazon
- Links to other books you've written
- Lists of books you recommend

Most sales are driven by reviews. Here are the steps in writing a review:

1. Find a book on your topic.
2. Make sure you have a profile and are a registered reviewer on Amazon.
3. Buy the book and read it.
4. Write a review.
5. Don't forget to mention your own book.

Amazon's potential is endless. In fact, you can establish an "author presence" through author pages, tags, keywords, discussions, Listmania, AmazonConnect, and your own author's profile. On the other hand, Amazon can be confusing and frustrating at first. Fortunately, the site is getting better at and more timely in responding to requests for help. There are so many benefits for authors, it is worth the trouble to learn your way around the site.

< 139 >

Articles

Make a list of publications that address your subject and query the editors about articles you will write at no charge. Articles boost your credibility as an expert on your subject and can be reproduced as promotional materials in your press kit. Your article should not be a commercial for your book; it should be what your consumers care about. Learn what the editor is looking for to address the publication's readers; then provide it. And don't forget about the myriad article sites on the Web. Use keywords to ensure that it will be found. Link to the appropriate page on your website.

Blogging

Approximately 150,000 new blogs are started every day. Some of them are never intended to be read by anyone but the blogger's family. Others find a small but devoted following. A few become nationally or even internationally read, such as The Huffington Post, TechCrunch, and Mashable! People blog for many reasons—to keep a kind of diary of events as they unfold; to reflect on various topics of interest to the blogger; to support a position, political or otherwise; to serve the needs of the blog's readers; to display their creative abilities; to market a brand or a product; and to entertain, educate, or enlighten. I'm sure I have barely scratched the surface. But for purposes of your book, you need to be very clear about the answers to this question.

Why should you blog?
1. To provide value to your readers

< 140 >

The first rule of having a presence on the Web is to create a benefit for anyone who lands on your site. Web surfers have short attention spans. There is so much to see and so little time. If they don't find a reason to read past your first line, they are gone in a click. The old WIIFM (what's in it for me?) applies. Most successful bloggers are generous. They give away lots of information. It is there for the taking, and it's all free.

2. To inform, teach, guide, entertain, or all of these

The content of that information is important because it relates to the mission of your blog. My blog, The Writing Life, is "full of musings, observations, and reflections of a 40-year veteran of the craft." Its purpose is to encourage writers to write, and it does that through information, tips on writing and running a freelance business, humor, and personal insights into a variety of topics related to writing.

3. To develop a following of loyal followers and raving fans

All writers crave readers. Bloggers certainly do. If you have what you think is a compelling message, naturally you want others to read it and become captivated. But one visit to your blog is not enough. You want readers to return, again and again. In fact, you want them to subscribe and have your blog land in their e-mail in-box every time you post. Your blog host does its part by providing RSS feeds and widgets to make subscribing easy. Learn about these tools, and take advantage of them.

< 141 >

4. To create and reinforce your brand

Branding products is not a new idea, but branding yourself may be. You are your brand, and everything you do, say, or write is a way to expose and expand awareness of your brand to many potential readers. Remember, *www* stands for World Wide Web. That means your message and the way it is presented are being broadcast all around the world. That is reason enough to put some time and effort into how you construct your blog, as well as each and every post.

5. To sell ideas, services, or products

Content counts. You have to have something to say, something worth reading. But WIIFM applies to you as well as your reader. You have products, even if they are only concepts, ideas, philosophies. If you're in business, what you are selling is more concrete. But even though selling is part of your purpose, if your blog is one big, online commercial, people may not find that worth too many return visits. Before you start designing your blog on WordPress, Blogger, or Godaddy, take some time to think about why you want a blog. It may be that you just need to emote or rant, but as business objectives those are unlikely to attract the kind of followers you want. Think of your blog as an equation: purpose + content + packaging = subscribers. That is a foolproof formula for successful blogging.

How do you learn about blogging?

Start by visiting blog directories and checking out the top-ranked blogs. Then, of course, check out blogs on your topic

< 142 >

or on writing. If you see something that rings your chimes, comment on it. If you really like it, let the blogger know.

What do you write about?

The list of topics is long and varied and depends a lot on who will be reading your blog. Alexandria K. Brown, "the Ezine Queen," suggests that you should answer questions you have been asked in the past. Ask yourself in what areas you would like people to think of you as a resource or an expert. Write about those areas. Think back to competitive titles on your subject or books you are reading now. Give brief reviews and recommend those you think are worthwhile.

How do you get your blog noticed?

Where will your blog fit in this crowded blogosphere? If you are seeking an audience beyond your family and friends, how will you find it? How will your little blog be noticed among the many thousand vying for attention?

1. *Put a link to your blog in your e-mail signature, every page of your website,* all outgoing correspondence, your newsletter, your author's blurb on articles, business cards, and anything you publish. For example, my e-mail signature includes "writeanonfictonbook.com/wordpress."

2. *Include RSS feeds so people can subscribe to your blog.* RSS (most commonly translated as "Really Simple Syndication") is a family of Web feed formats used to publish

< 143 >

frequently updated works, such as blog entries and news headlines. Popular RSS feeds include Google, Yahoo, Bloglines, and Netvibes.

3. *Use trackback links when you quote from or refer to other blog posts.* A trackback is one of three types of methods for Web authors to request notification when somebody links to one of their documents. This enables authors to keep track of who is linking to their blogs.

4. *Respond to comments readers make on your blog. Have a conversation.* Often, this will take you in directions you could never have imagined. Blogging is interactive in that way. If your blog is static, it defeats its purpose of engaging readers.

5. *Create tags for every blog post so that search engines can find your blog.* A tag is a keyword or term assigned to a piece of information (such as an Internet bookmark, digital image, or computer file). Use the same tags in all blogs you write on the same topics. For example, if you write about blogs, use tags such as *blogs, blogging,* and *blog posts.*

6. *Create a "best posts page" category on your main page; link to your best posts.* Blog posts tend to become lost or forgotten as the months go by. Read through your previously published posts, and choose several that still have relevance and resonance. Remember to repeat the same tags.

< 144 >

7. *You are a resource; provide value.* Web surfers have notoriously short attention spans. If they happen to land at your blog site and don't find anything useful, they will move on, never to return. They certainly won't register for your RSS feed. But if you consistently give readers something of interest they can use, they may become followers and raving fans.

What are the top ten great blogs about blogging?
1. Problogger
2. Copyblogger
3. Blog Squad
4. Guy Kawasaki
5. John Chow
6. Daily Blog Tips
7. Dosh Dosh
8. Weblog Tools Collection
9. Blog Herald
10. Blogging Pro

Book clubs
There is one for every different need. Go to each website, and download guidelines for submission. The questions you must answer are, Why should they buy your book? How can you help them serve their customers better?

Book fairs
There are international, national, regional, and local book fairs. The best thing about them is that you meet a lot of

< 145 >

interesting people. But don't go to a fair expecting to make money selling your book. Exhibiting is expensive, even at a small fair. You should consider carefully whether you want to spend your promotional funds that way.

Bookstores

Compile a list of local bookstores and visit them, book in hand. Offer to do a workshop, a presentation, or a signing. Help with promotion of the event, and cooperate with the community relations person in any way you can. The bookstore is in business to sell books; your job is to help it sell yours. Don't just think of the big chains; think small. If there are locally owned bookstores in your city, introduce yourself, and patronize them. They are usually happy to feature local authors. In St. Louis, four such stores—Subterranean Books, Left Bank Books, Pudd'nhead Books, and Main Street Books—have just formed an alliance that is doing exciting things "to support the creative and literary efforts in our city."

Nontraditional sales

- Bookstores are not the only places to sell books, nor are they necessarily the best places. Other places are called "nontraditional sales." As the author, you reap all the profits from most of them.
- Bookstores get a substantial discount, which cuts into your profits.
- Your book has great potential for spin-off products.
- Sell not just your book, but your message as well.

< 146 >

- Send free books, three-dimensional business cards, gifts, or marketing materials to associations, organizations, meetings of any kind, and libraries. Submit your book for inclusion in catalogs.
- Sell your books in the back of the room when you give presentations or workshops.

Public relations

Prepare a professional-looking press kit. Paste the cover of your book on the front of the pocket folder. Inside, put a press release, an information sheet about your book, an author's bio and photo, talking points to be used in interviews, and contact and ordering information.

Give away premiums that display your book's cover.

On your website, set up a media page. Think of it as a press kit, and create links to all of the above items. Make it easy for people to download a usable press release, photo, and any other information.

Social networking

Word of mouth is a powerful marketing technique, no matter what you're trying to promote. Join appropriate associations for self-publishers, marketers, professional speakers, and those that cater to people interested in your topic. And, of course, network online. By 2012 more than *1 billion* people are expected to be online through blogs, social networks, or photo/video sharing services. Every day new sites are launched to enable people to broaden their conversations. This is networking on a scale few of us could ever

< 147 >

have imagined. What follows are the "giants of the social networking scene."

- **MySpace** started out as the exclusive domain of young people, and after trying to become a mainstream site, went back to its roots. MySpace was the first social network to make the word *friends* (meaning contacts) part of our everyday language. While MySpace members aren't as old or sophisticated as Facebook users, they function seamlessly in their own piece of cyberspace. If you are an adult who insists on being on MySpace, ask your teenager to help you.

- **Facebook** is the biggest social networking site. Forty percent of its members are over thirty-five. Facebook offers personal profiles, calendars, movie reviews, photos, groups for every conceivable interest, targeted advertising, demographic profiling, and multiple ways to keep in touch. Members use Facebook to keep up with friends and friends of friends. It now also provides "business pages" for setting up professional and business profiles.

- **LinkedIn** is the number one social network for businesspeople and professionals. The site works on the principle of six degrees of separation. Members find and connect to their existing business contacts and then to their contacts' contacts. Members post resumes, form networks, write recommendations, and keep their contacts updated on changes in their professional lives. When members update

< 148 >

their profiles, their new information becomes immediately available to everyone in their networks.

- **Twitter** is an innovative, free social network that restricts messages to 140 characters. "Tweets" range from "what I'm doing right this minute" to trends and important issues. More than 100 services have sprung up that mimic Twitter, and there are many sites that augment its services. Followers can tune in to messages from other members and send targeted messages to people they follow by simply putting @ in front of the other person's Twitter name.

- **YouTube** is the best-known and most popular video site. It was acquired by Google in 2006 and went mainstream in 2007, appealing to both individuals and businesses. Members upload more than 65,000 videos a day. Most social networks and websites support video. As a social networking site, YouTube features personal spaces, playlists, friends, favorites, and conversations.

Speaking engagements

Most people shake in their boots at the very thought of speaking in public. Yet, as a writer, chances are you will find yourself in front of an audience sooner or later. The ability to speak confidently and comfortably to a group will help you communicate your knowledge in an engaging style, enhance your credibility, and build self-confidence. Position yourself as an expert, and line up speaking engagements at no charge. The opportunities are practically endless: civic

< 149 >

groups, business and trade associations, Rotary clubs, and local libraries, to name a few.

Public speaking is a learnable skill. There are four simple guidelines for giving an effective talk, no matter what its purpose or the size of the audience.

1. Prepare

You must prepare for any spoken encounter, even if you have only seconds to do so. In the case of a "prepared speech," you are expected to think it through before you speak. The audience has a purpose for being there, and it is incumbent upon you to know the subject matter and be able to present it in an easy-to-follow manner.

There is an art to speaking to every single person in the audience. No matter how many people are in the room, your job is to make every one of them feel like the most important person there. You can do that by preparing your presentation as if it were a conversation with one other person.

Finally, visual aids can enrich your talk, or they can wreck it. If you are planning to use any, it's important to be very familiar with them, whether they include equipment, charts, handouts, or a blackboard. Do not leave your visual aids to chance.

2. Practice

There is no acceptable reason for not practicing, but there are consequences when you don't do it. For one thing, lack of practice shows. For another, it undermines your credibility as an expert. In addition, lack of practice reveals

< 150 >

character flaws and sloppy work habits; it fails to meet the needs of your audience; and it casts doubt on how well you know your subject.

The first time you give a presentation in public should never be the first time. Go over the actual sequence again and again. Listen to yourself on a tape recorder. You may be shocked to hear how you sound to others. Pace your words so that you are not speaking too fast or too slowly. Breathe deeply, which will relax you and deepen the tonal quality of your voice. Use gestures and movements to add emphasis to the points you want people to remember. If you can, video-tape yourself, or practice in front of people. Then, hard as this may be, ask for feedback.

3. Present

The heart of the matter, of course, is what you say and how you say it. Think of your talk as a package. Content is what is inside. It is your message, and it must be substantive and accurate. Delivery and appearance are the packaging. No one will bother with what you say if the way you say it or the way you look turns people off. Your posture makes an instant impression and influences your audience's perceptions throughout your presentation.

Before you begin your presentation, take a few moments to center yourself. Every person's centering technique is unique. If you don't already have one, take time to discover this valuable resource in yourself. You'll probably find many other times to use it besides public speaking. If you have done steps one and two, your presentation should be a piece

< 151 >

of cake. The only element you can't control is your audience, but you can manage it.

Of course, you hope your audience is interested and attentive, but if you are plagued with challengers or talkers, there are diplomatic though firm ways to handle them. When someone wants to tell you and everyone else everything he or she knows, treat that person with firmness, care, respect, and acceptance. Annoying as problem people can be, when you find yourself confronting one, don't lose sight of that person's feelings and your own need to deal with them in a constructive manner.

4. Process
After each presentation, it's important for you to evaluate your performance so that you can learn from it. Processing has two steps: self-evaluation and feedback. If you do receive evaluation forms, don't look at them until you have asked yourself these questions: What did I do today in my presentation that worked? What did I do today in my presentation that did not work? If I were to do the same presentation tomorrow, what would I change?

Successful presentations don't just happen. They are not the result of luck or innate talent. Presentation skills are learned and earned by those who prepare, practice, present, and process effectively.

Specialty retailers
Research stores and sites that sell special-interest books and products that are related to your topic. For example, if

< 152 >

your topic is camping, REI would be a perfect venue for you. Visit them with copies of your book.

Websites

Here are ten characteristics of a great website:

1. A memorable identity: Develop a consistent message.
2. New content: Change something on your website at least once a month—headline, special offer, posts.
3. Something of value: Make content informative, entertaining, inspirational, educational, or provocative. Give stuff away.
4. Appeal to search engines: Use meta tags and keywords to help search engines and Web surfers find you.
5. Link exchanges: Find complementary sites; link to them; ask them to link to you.
6. Interactivity: Provide a way for visitors to comment.
7. Consistency: Be sure your social media identity reflects the real you.
8. Graphics: A picture is worth 1,000 words; 1,000 words are too many for Web surfers.
9. Ease of bookmarking: Use widgets to bookmark certain Web pages to Digg, StumbleUpon, and Sphinn.
10. Capture e-mail addresses: Use a mailing list service to collect e-mail addresses to send out announcements, special offers, or a newsletter.

< 153 >

Promotion Details Worksheet

Advance review copies (Who? When? Where?)

Advertising (Media? Size or length? Cost? Contact? Deadline?)

Amazon.com (Possibilities?)

Article (Publications? Editors? Subject? Length? Deadline?)

Book clubs (General interest? Specialty?)

< 154 >

Book fairs (Location? Sponsors? Dates? Fees? Displays? Deadline?)

Bookstores (Chains? Privately owned? Distributor? Discount? Location?)

Direct marketing (Pieces? Design? Mailing list? Cost? Postage? Dates?)

Elevator speech (Who? What? Benefit?)

Internet marketing (Website? Social networking sites? Amazon?)

< 155 >

Networking (Organizations? Events? Dates? Locations? Fees?)

Nontraditional sales (Spin-off products? Selling your message?)

Press kit (Contents? Design? Printing? Media?)

Public relations (Package? Premiums? Catalogs? Online media room?)

Speaking engagements (Organizations? Bookstores? Subject? Contact?)

< 156 >

Specialty retailers (Stores? Websites? Associations?)

Website (Designer? Host? Search engines? Tracking results? Cost?)

< 157 >

RECOMMENDED READING

On Writing

Bird by Bird: Some Instructions on Writing and Life
Anne Lamott

On Writing
Stephen King

On Writing Well
William Zinsser

poemcrazy: freeing your life with words
Susan Goldsmith Wooldridge

The Right to Write: An Invitation and Initiation into the Writing Life
Julia Cameron

< 159 >

The Writing Life
Annie Dillard

Words To Live By: Reflections on the writing life from a 40-year veteran
Bobbi Linkemer

Writing Alone and with Others
Pat Schneider

Writing Down the Bones: Freeing the Writer Within
Natalie Goldberg

Writing About Your Life: a Journey into the Past
William Zinsser

On Words
QPB Dictionary of Difficult Words

Roget's Super Thesaurus

Roget's International Thesaurus

Webster's New Collegiate Dictionary

Oxford American Writer's Thesaurus

< 160 >

On Style and Grammar

Eats, Shoots and Leaves: The Zero Tolerance Approach to Punctuation
Lynn Truss

Elements of Style
William Strunk Jr. and E.B. White

The Chicago Manual of Style, 16th Edition

The New York Times Manual of Style and Usage

Woe Is I: The Grammarphobe's Guide to Better English in Plain English
Patricia T. O'Conner

Words Fail Me: What Everyone Who Writes Should Know About Writing
Patricia T. O'Conner

Words into Type
Prentice Hall

On Enriching Writing

1,911 Best Things Anybody Ever Said
Robert Byrne

< 161 >

2,715 One-Line Quotations for Speakers, Writers & Raconteurs
Edward F. Murphy

Bartlett's Familiar Quotations
John Bartlett and Justin Kaplan

Oxford Dictionary of Phrase, Saying, & Quotation
Susan Ratcliffe

Sun Signs for Writers
Bev Walton-Porter

Two Jews, Three Opinions: A Collectiom of 20th Century American Jewish Quotations
Sandee Branwarsky and Deborah Mark

On Freelancing

Ghost Writing for Fun & Profit
Eva Shaw, PhD

Going Solo: How to Survive & Thrive as a Freelance Writer (e-book)
Bobbi Linkemer

How to Write a Nonfiction Book: From Concept to Completion in 6 Months, (Kindle edition)
Bobbi Linkemer

< 162 >

Invisible Author: Confessions of a Ghostwriter (e-book)
Bobbi Linkemer

Secrets of a Freelance Writer: How to Make $100,000 a Year or More, Third Edition
Robert W. Bly

Successful Freelancing: The Complete Guide to Establishing and Running Any Kind of Freelance Business
Marian Faux

Writing Nonfiction: Turning Thoughts into Books
Dan Poynter

On Publishing

Business and Legal Forms for Authors and Self-publishers
Tad Crawford

The Complete Guide to Self-publishing: Everything You Need to Know to Write, Publish, Promote, and Sell Your Book
Marilyn Ross and Sue Collier

How to Get a Literary Agent
Michael Larsen

How to Get Your Book Published: An Insider's Guide
Herbert W. Bell

< 163 >

How to Publish, Promote and Sell Your Own Book
Robert Lawrence Holt

How to Write a Book Proposal
Michael Larsen

The Insider's Guide to Getting an Agent
Lori Perkins

Nonfiction Book Proposals Anybody Can Write
Elizabeth Lyon

*Dan Poynter's Self-publishing Manual: How to Write,
Print and Sell Your Own Book*
Dan Poynter

Self-Publishing Success Secrets 101
Bob Baker

*The Well-Fed Self-Publisher: How to Turn One Book into a
Full-Time Living*
Peter Bowerman

Write the Perfect Book Proposal: 10 That Sold and Why
Jeff Herman and Deborah Adams

*The Fine Print of Self-publishing: Everything You Need to
Know About the Costs, Contracts, and Process of Self-
publishing,* Fourth Edition
Mark Levine

< 164 >

On Promoting

55 Ways to Promote & Sell Your Book on the Internet
Bob Baker

1001 Ways to Market Your Books
John Kremer

Beyond the Bookstore
Brian Jud

A Survival Guide to Social Media and Web 2.0 Optimization: Strategies, Tactics, and Tools for Succeeding in the Social Web
Deltina Hay

The Huffington Post Complete Guide to Blogging
The Editors of the Huffington Post

Guerrilla Marketing for Writers: 100 No-Cost, Low-Cost Weapons for Selling Your Work
Jay Conrad Levinson, Rick Frishman, Michael Larsen, and David Hancock

Publicity for Nonprofits: Generating Media Exposure That Leads to Awareness, Growth, and Contributions
Sandra Beckwith

Red Hot Internet Publicity: An Insider's Guide to Promoting Your Book on the Internet
Penny C. Sansevieri

< 165 >

Secrets of Social Media Marketing: How to Use Online Conversations to Turbo-charge Your Business
Paul Gillin

< 166 >

INDEX

< 167 >

< 168 >

< 169 >

< 170 >

< 171 >

< 172 >

< 173 >

L

M

< 174 >

< 175 >

< 176 >

< 177 >

< 178 >

< 179 >

< 180 >

< 181 >

23647866R00110

Printed in Poland
by Amazon Fulfillment
Poland Sp. z o.o., Wrocław